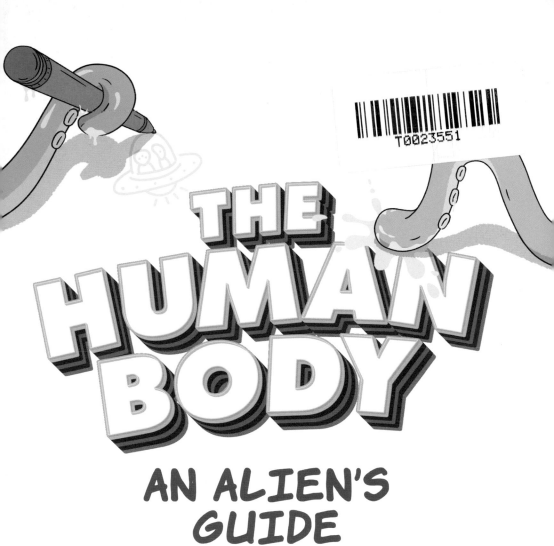

THE HUMAN BODY

AN ALIEN'S GUIDE

LEANDRO CUNHA

RUTH REDFORD
ALSO BY ZAG AND ZOG

MAYO CLINIC PRESS KIDS

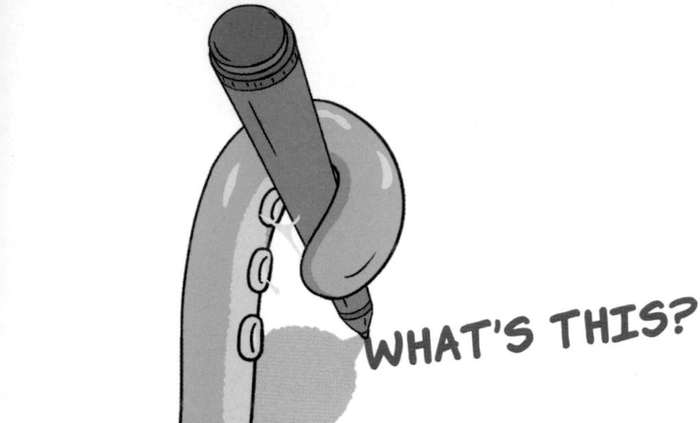
WHAT'S THIS?

With gratitude to Khaled S. Mohammed, MB, BCh

MAYO CLINIC PRESS KIDS | An imprint of Mayo Clinic Press
200 First St. SW
Rochester, MN 55905
mcpress.mayoclinic.org
To stay informed about Mayo Clinic Press, please subscribe to our free e-newsletter at mcpress.mayoclinic.org or follow us on social media.

For bulk sales contact Mayo Clinic at SpecialSalesMayoBooks@mayo.edu.

Proceeds from the sale of every book benefit important medical research and education at Mayo Clinic.

ISBN: 9798887701424 (library binding) | 9798887701462 (paperback)
9798887701448 ebook | 9798887701455 (multiuser PDF)
9798887701479 (multiuser ePub3)

Library of Congress Control Number: 2023947058

SPACESHIP LOG
TABLE OF CONTENTS

SPACESHIP LOG:

WELCOME TO THE HUMAN BODY

ZOG: WELCOME TO THE ZOG LOG. IT'S DAY 5,348 OF OUR SEARCH FOR OTHER PLANETARY LIFE-FORMS.

ZAG: ZOG, I THOUGHT WE WERE GOING TO CALL IT THE ZAG-ZOG LOG?

ZOG: ...WELCOME TO THE ZAG-ZOG LOG! SEE? IT'S NOT AS CATCHY! LOOK! WE'VE FINALLY FOUND SOMETHING.

ZAG: LIFE OUTSIDE PLANET CORPUS?!

ZOG: LET'S TAKE A CLOSER LOOK. ZAG, START THE REACTOR!

ZAG: AFFIRMATIVE!

ZOG: I HOPE IT'S NOT GOING TO BE STICKY.

ZAG: OR SLIMY! YUCK! UM, WHAT IS THAT?

ZOG: A LIFE-FORM, I THINK.

ZAG: IT'S TERRIFYING!

ZOG: SHOULD WE PHONE HOME?

HQ: COME IN, COME IN.

ZOG: COPY! ZOG HERE! WE'VE FOUND A STRANGE LIFE-FORM.

ZAG: ...AND ZAG TOO! ZAG COPIES!

HQ: FIND OUT ABOUT THEM, BUT STAY UNDER THE RADAR.

ZAG: NO RADARS HERE!

ZOG: THEY MEAN STAY UNDER COVER. USE THE SHRINKING SUITS.

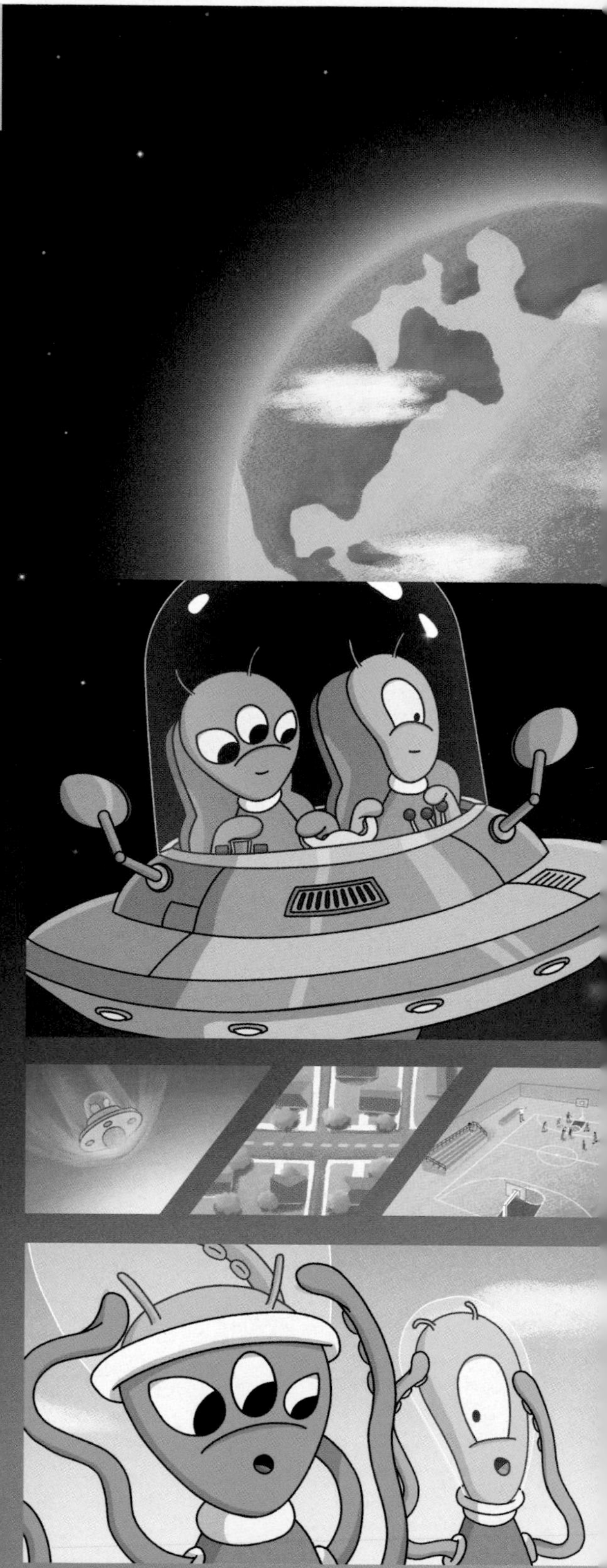

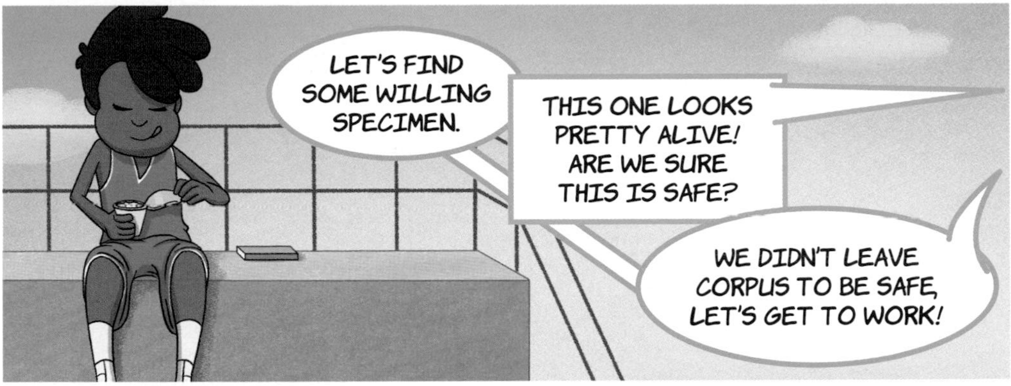
LET'S FIND SOME WILLING SPECIMEN.
THIS ONE LOOKS PRETTY ALIVE! ARE WE SURE THIS IS SAFE?
WE DIDN'T LEAVE CORPUS TO BE SAFE, LET'S GET TO WORK!

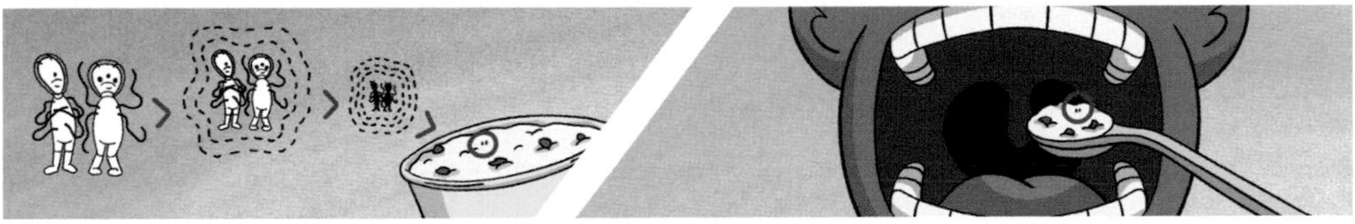

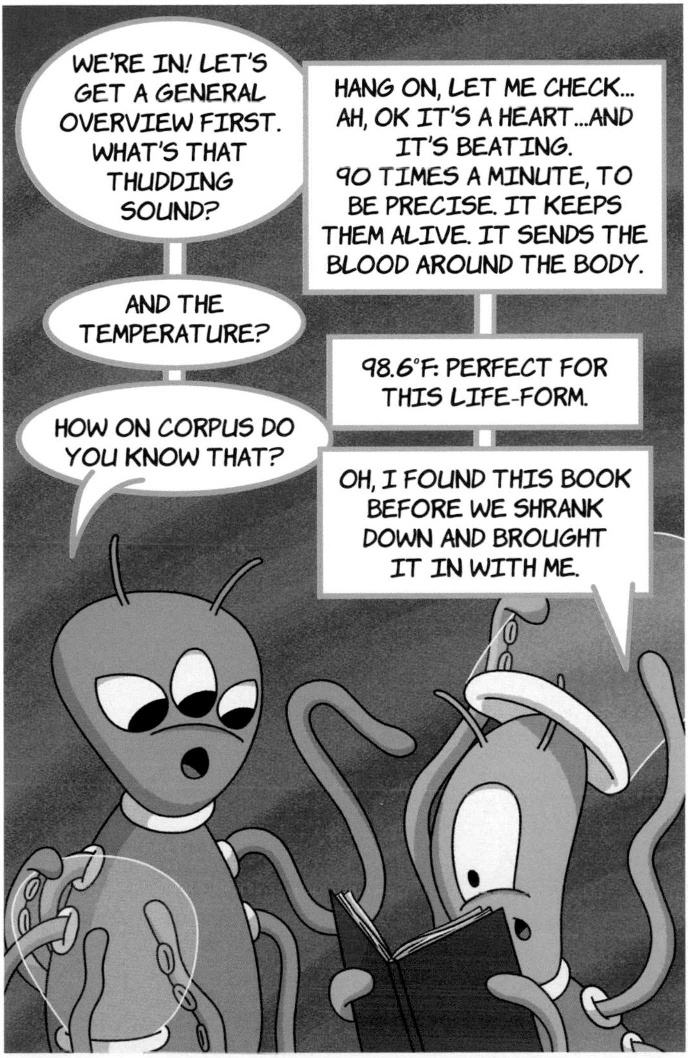
WE'RE IN! LET'S GET A GENERAL OVERVIEW FIRST. WHAT'S THAT THUDDING SOUND?
HANG ON, LET ME CHECK... AH, OK IT'S A HEART...AND IT'S BEATING. 90 TIMES A MINUTE, TO BE PRECISE. IT KEEPS THEM ALIVE. IT SENDS THE BLOOD AROUND THE BODY.
AND THE TEMPERATURE?
98.6°F: PERFECT FOR THIS LIFE-FORM.
HOW ON CORPUS DO YOU KNOW THAT?
OH, I FOUND THIS BOOK BEFORE WE SHRANK DOWN AND BROUGHT IT IN WITH ME.

CHECK IT OUT!

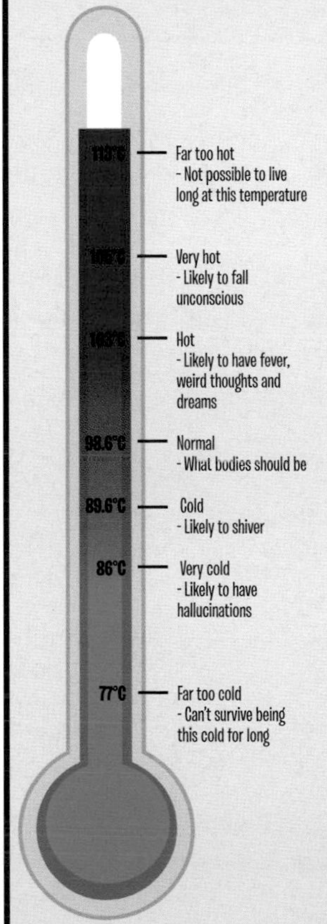
Far too hot
- Not possible to live long at this temperature
Very hot
- Likely to fall unconscious
Hot
- Likely to have fever, weird thoughts and dreams
98.6°C
Normal
- What bodies should be
89.6°C
Cold
- Likely to shiver
86°C
Very cold
- Likely to have hallucinations
77°C
Far too cold
- Can't survive being this cold for long

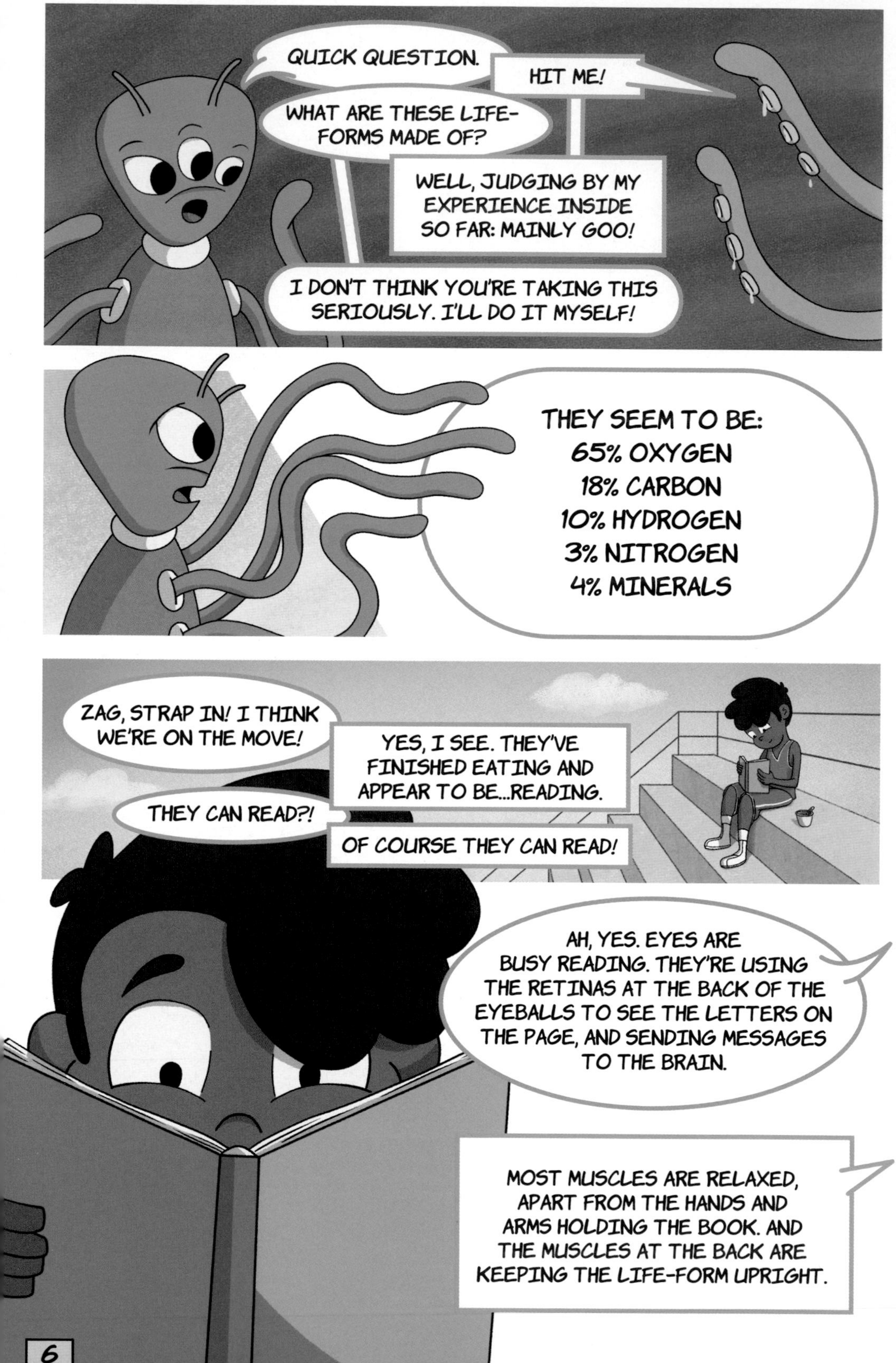
QUICK QUESTION.
HIT ME!
WHAT ARE THESE LIFE-FORMS MADE OF?
WELL, JUDGING BY MY EXPERIENCE INSIDE SO FAR: MAINLY GOO!
I DON'T THINK YOU'RE TAKING THIS SERIOUSLY. I'LL DO IT MYSELF!
THEY SEEM TO BE: 65% OXYGEN 18% CARBON 10% HYDROGEN 3% NITROGEN 4% MINERALS
ZAG, STRAP IN! I THINK WE'RE ON THE MOVE!
YES, I SEE. THEY'VE FINISHED EATING AND APPEAR TO BE...READING.
THEY CAN READ?!
OF COURSE THEY CAN READ!
AH, YES. EYES ARE BUSY READING. THEY'RE USING THE RETINAS AT THE BACK OF THE EYEBALLS TO SEE THE LETTERS ON THE PAGE, AND SENDING MESSAGES TO THE BRAIN.
MOST MUSCLES ARE RELAXED, APART FROM THE HANDS AND ARMS HOLDING THE BOOK. AND THE MUSCLES AT THE BACK ARE KEEPING THE LIFE-FORM UPRIGHT.

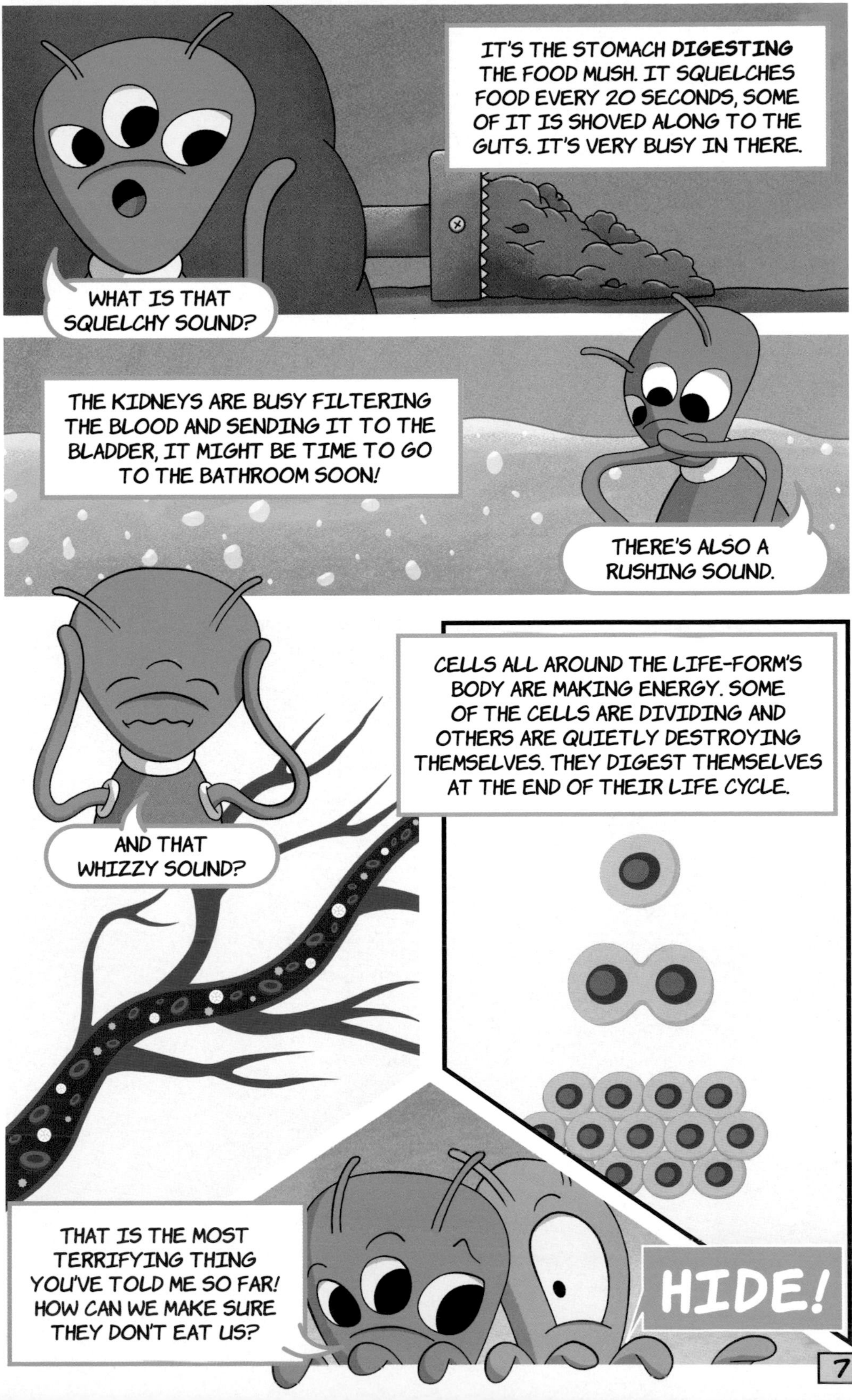

IT'S THE STOMACH **DIGESTING** THE FOOD MUSH. IT SQUELCHES FOOD EVERY 20 SECONDS, SOME OF IT IS SHOVED ALONG TO THE GUTS. IT'S VERY BUSY IN THERE.

WHAT IS THAT SQUELCHY SOUND?

THE KIDNEYS ARE BUSY FILTERING THE BLOOD AND SENDING IT TO THE BLADDER, IT MIGHT BE TIME TO GO TO THE BATHROOM SOON!

THERE'S ALSO A RUSHING SOUND.

AND THAT WHIZZY SOUND?

CELLS ALL AROUND THE LIFE-FORM'S BODY ARE MAKING ENERGY. SOME OF THE CELLS ARE DIVIDING AND OTHERS ARE QUIETLY DESTROYING THEMSELVES. THEY DIGEST THEMSELVES AT THE END OF THEIR LIFE CYCLE.

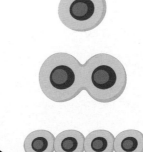

THAT IS THE MOST TERRIFYING THING YOU'VE TOLD ME SO FAR! HOW CAN WE MAKE SURE THEY DON'T EAT US?

HIDE!

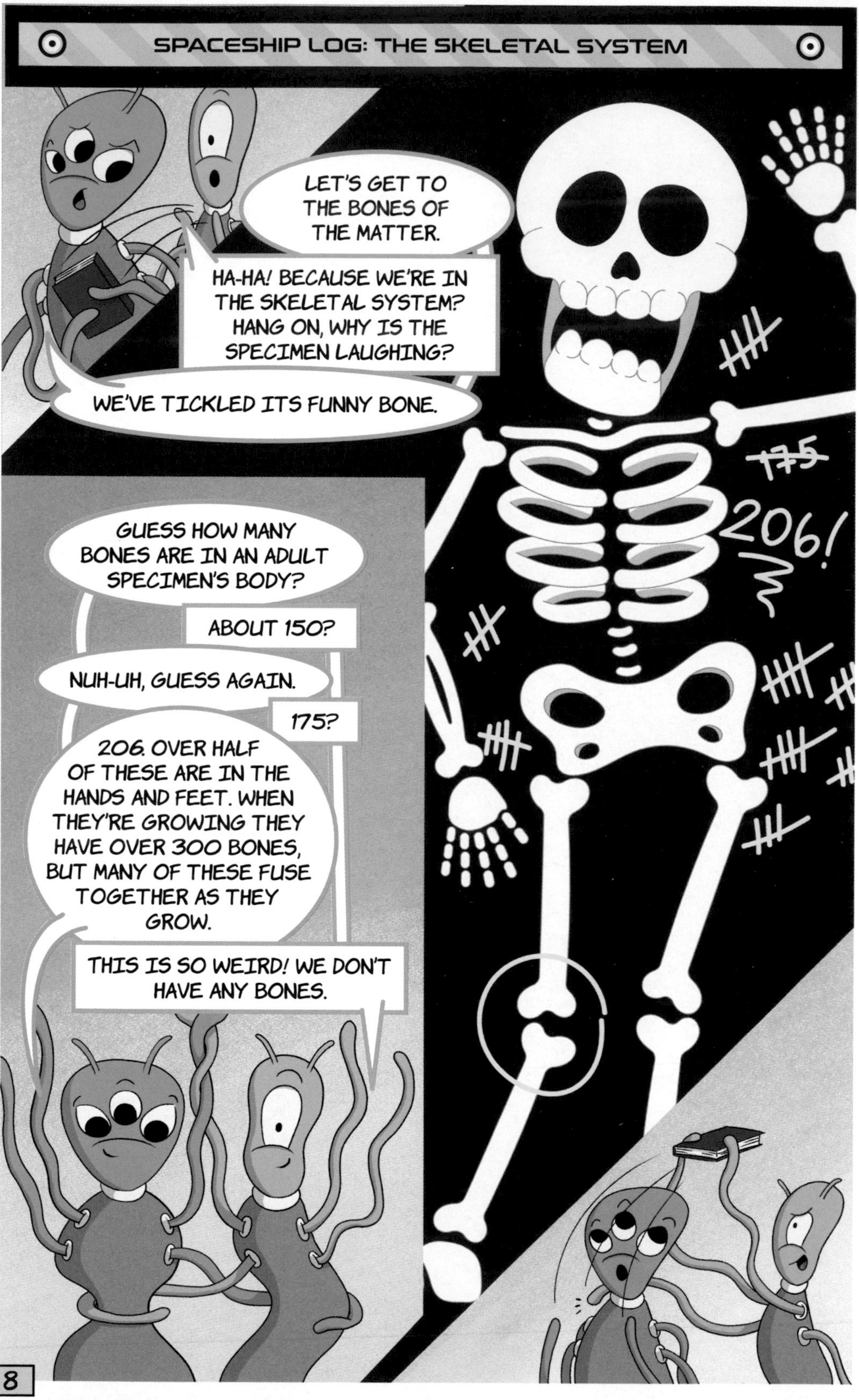
SPACESHIP LOG: THE SKELETAL SYSTEM
LET'S GET TO THE BONES OF THE MATTER.
HA-HA! BECAUSE WE'RE IN THE SKELETAL SYSTEM? HANG ON, WHY IS THE SPECIMEN LAUGHING?
WE'VE TICKLED ITS FUNNY BONE.
175
206!
GUESS HOW MANY BONES ARE IN AN ADULT SPECIMEN'S BODY?
ABOUT 150?
NUH-UH, GUESS AGAIN.
175?
206. OVER HALF OF THESE ARE IN THE HANDS AND FEET. WHEN THEY'RE GROWING THEY HAVE OVER 300 BONES, BUT MANY OF THESE FUSE TOGETHER AS THEY GROW.
THIS IS SO WEIRD! WE DON'T HAVE ANY BONES.

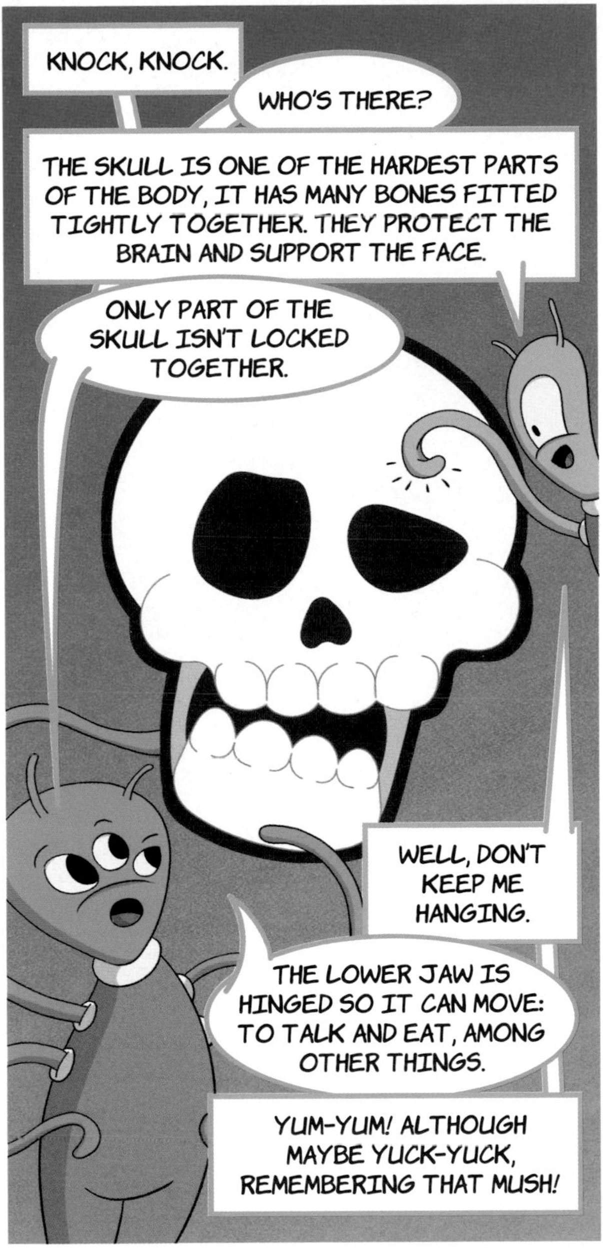
KNOCK, KNOCK.
WHO'S THERE?
THE SKULL IS ONE OF THE HARDEST PARTS OF THE BODY, IT HAS MANY BONES FITTED TIGHTLY TOGETHER. THEY PROTECT THE BRAIN AND SUPPORT THE FACE.
ONLY PART OF THE SKULL ISN'T LOCKED TOGETHER.
WELL, DON'T KEEP ME HANGING.
THE LOWER JAW IS HINGED SO IT CAN MOVE: TO TALK AND EAT, AMONG OTHER THINGS.
YUM-YUM! ALTHOUGH MAYBE YUCK-YUCK, REMEMBERING THAT MUSH!

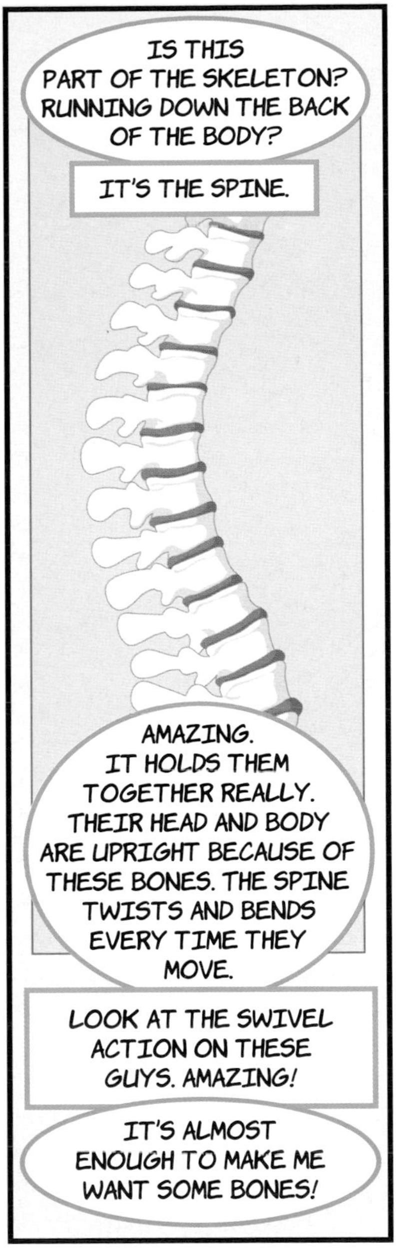
IS THIS PART OF THE SKELETON? RUNNING DOWN THE BACK OF THE BODY?
IT'S THE SPINE.
AMAZING. IT HOLDS THEM TOGETHER REALLY. THEIR HEAD AND BODY ARE UPRIGHT BECAUSE OF THESE BONES. THE SPINE TWISTS AND BENDS EVERY TIME THEY MOVE.
LOOK AT THE SWIVEL ACTION ON THESE GUYS. AMAZING!
IT'S ALMOST ENOUGH TO MAKE ME WANT SOME BONES!

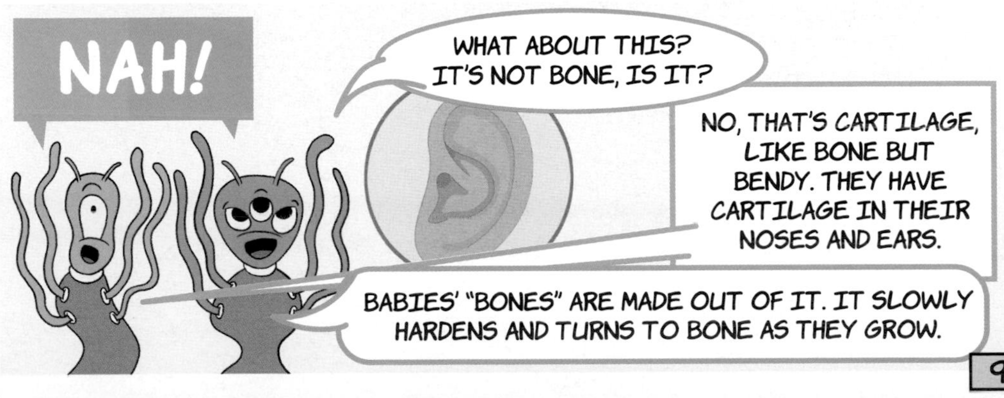
NAH!
WHAT ABOUT THIS? IT'S NOT BONE, IS IT?
NO, THAT'S CARTILAGE, LIKE BONE BUT BENDY. THEY HAVE CARTILAGE IN THEIR NOSES AND EARS.
BABIES' "BONES" ARE MADE OUT OF IT. IT SLOWLY HARDENS AND TURNS TO BONE AS THEY GROW.

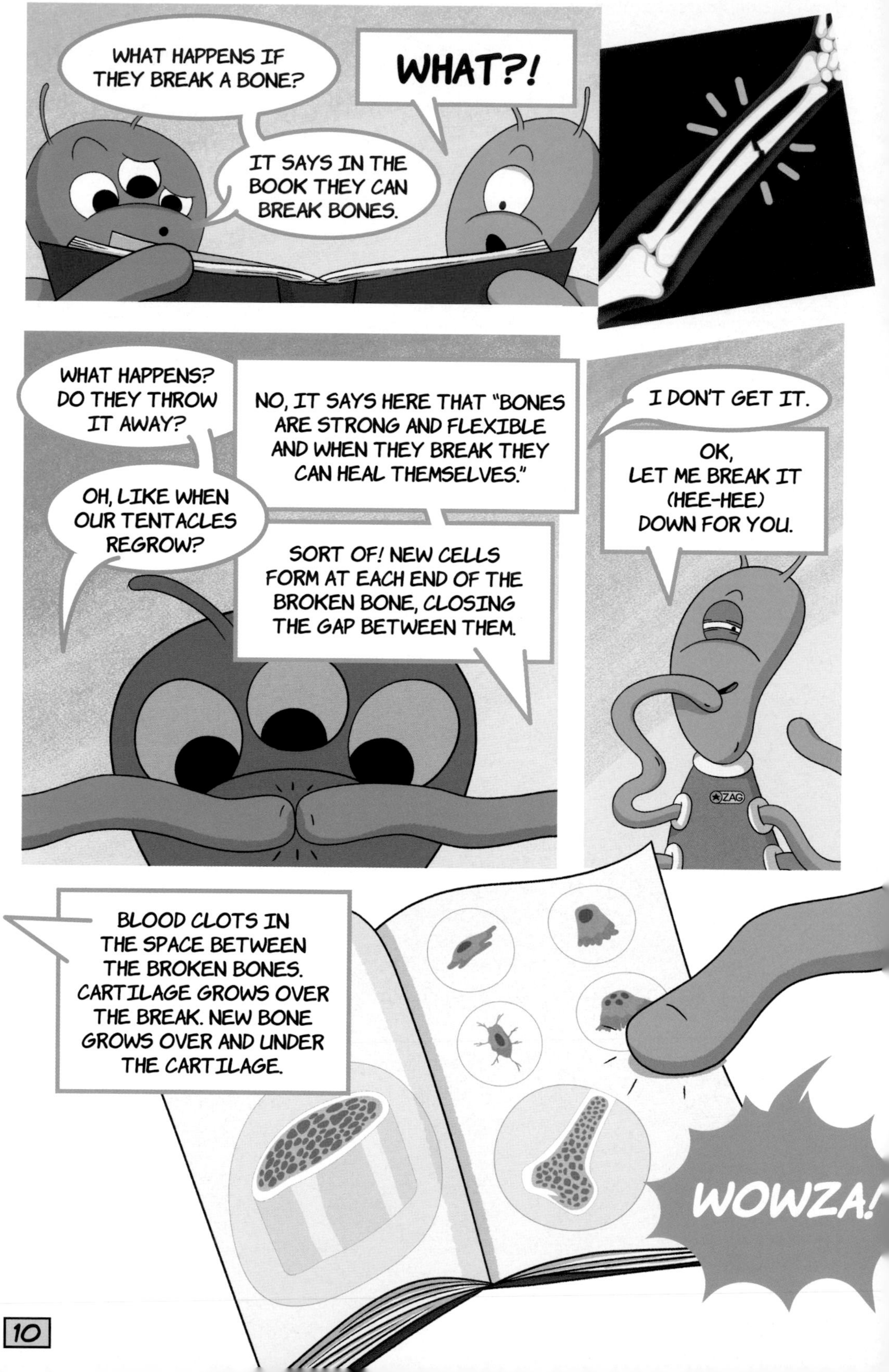
WHAT HAPPENS IF THEY BREAK A BONE?
WHAT?!
IT SAYS IN THE BOOK THEY CAN BREAK BONES.
WHAT HAPPENS? DO THEY THROW IT AWAY?
NO, IT SAYS HERE THAT "BONES ARE STRONG AND FLEXIBLE AND WHEN THEY BREAK THEY CAN HEAL THEMSELVES."
OH, LIKE WHEN OUR TENTACLES REGROW?
SORT OF! NEW CELLS FORM AT EACH END OF THE BROKEN BONE, CLOSING THE GAP BETWEEN THEM.
I DON'T GET IT.
OK, LET ME BREAK IT (HEE-HEE) DOWN FOR YOU.
ZAG
BLOOD CLOTS IN THE SPACE BETWEEN THE BROKEN BONES. CARTILAGE GROWS OVER THE BREAK. NEW BONE GROWS OVER AND UNDER THE CARTILAGE.
WOWZA!

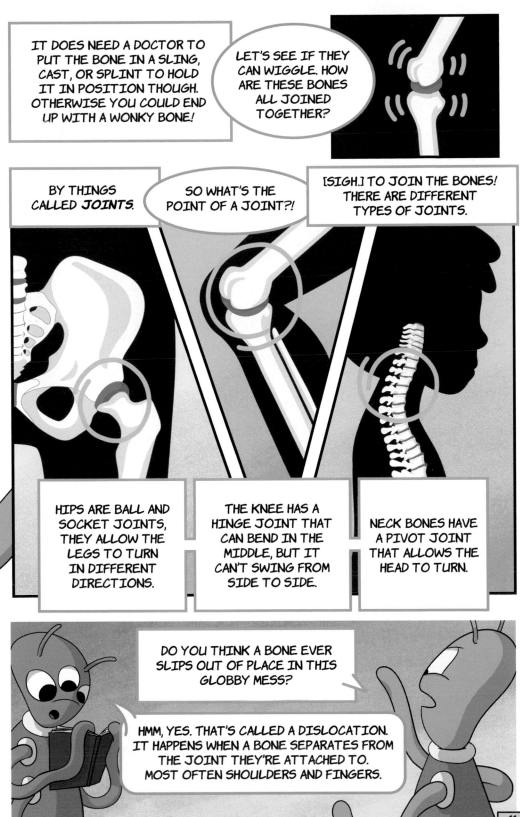

IT DOES NEED A DOCTOR TO PUT THE BONE IN A SLING, CAST, OR SPLINT TO HOLD IT IN POSITION THOUGH. OTHERWISE YOU COULD END UP WITH A WONKY BONE!

LET'S SEE IF THEY CAN WIGGLE. HOW ARE THESE BONES ALL JOINED TOGETHER?

BY THINGS CALLED **JOINTS**.

SO WHAT'S THE POINT OF A JOINT?!

[SIGH.] TO JOIN THE BONES! THERE ARE DIFFERENT TYPES OF JOINTS.

HIPS ARE BALL AND SOCKET JOINTS, THEY ALLOW THE LEGS TO TURN IN DIFFERENT DIRECTIONS.

THE KNEE HAS A HINGE JOINT THAT CAN BEND IN THE MIDDLE, BUT IT CAN'T SWING FROM SIDE TO SIDE.

NECK BONES HAVE A PIVOT JOINT THAT ALLOWS THE HEAD TO TURN.

DO YOU THINK A BONE EVER SLIPS OUT OF PLACE IN THIS GLOBBY MESS?

HMM, YES. THAT'S CALLED A DISLOCATION. IT HAPPENS WHEN A BONE SEPARATES FROM THE JOINT THEY'RE ATTACHED TO. MOST OFTEN SHOULDERS AND FINGERS.

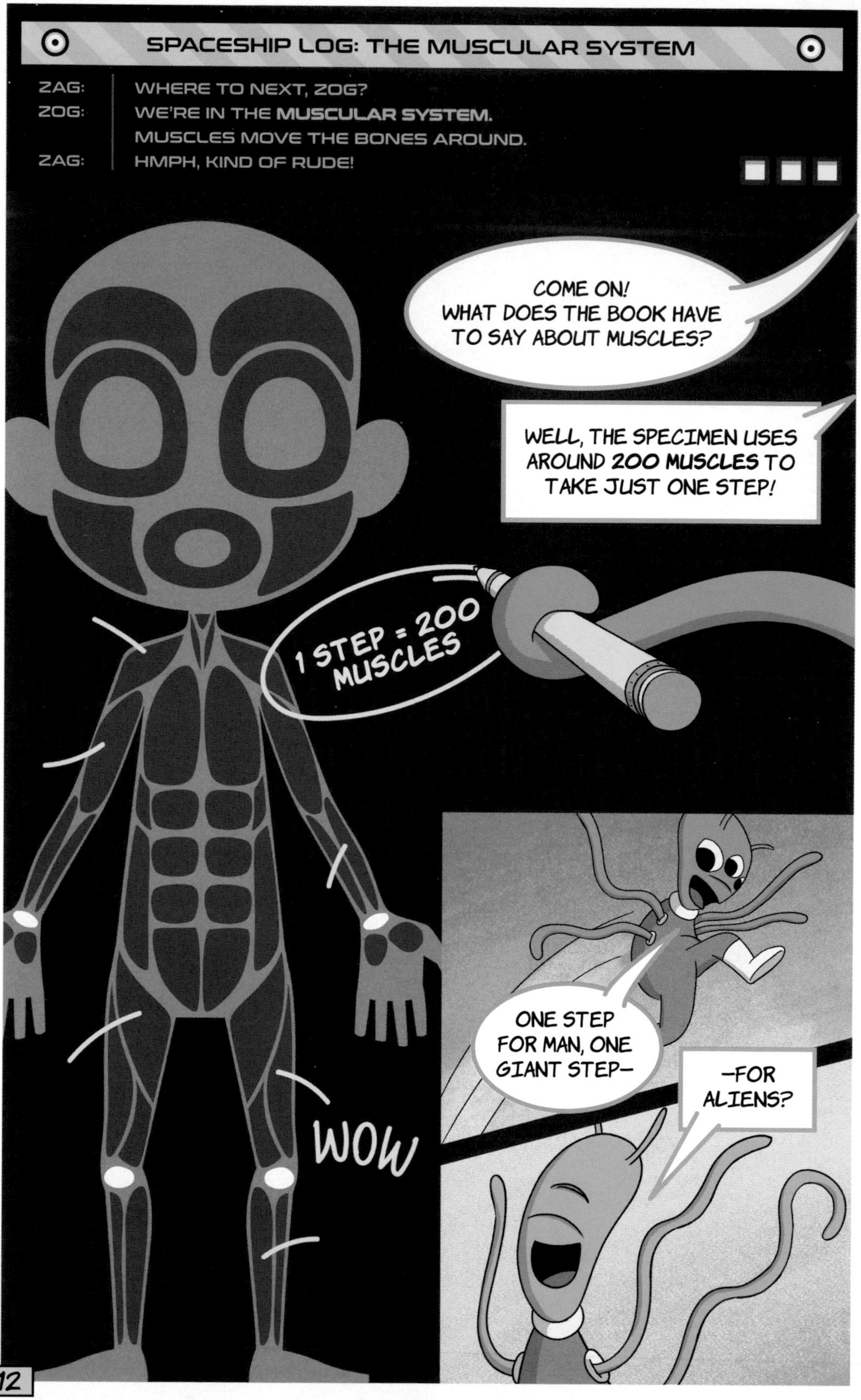
SPACESHIP LOG: THE MUSCULAR SYSTEM
ZAG: WHERE TO NEXT, ZOG?
ZOG: WE'RE IN THE MUSCULAR SYSTEM.
MUSCLES MOVE THE BONES AROUND.
ZAG: HMPH, KIND OF RUDE!
COME ON! WHAT DOES THE BOOK HAVE TO SAY ABOUT MUSCLES?
WELL, THE SPECIMEN USES AROUND 200 MUSCLES TO TAKE JUST ONE STEP!
1 STEP = 200 MUSCLES
WOW
ONE STEP FOR MAN, ONE GIANT STEP—
—FOR ALIENS?

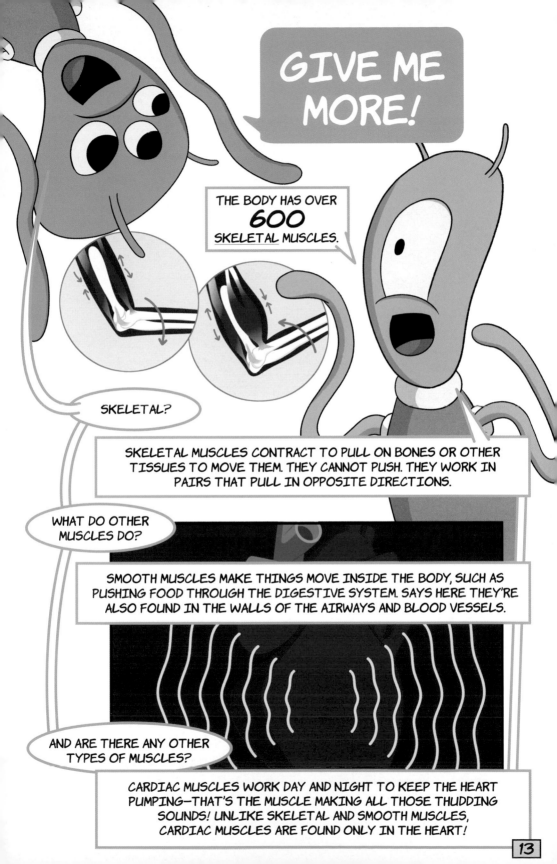

GIVE ME MORE!

THE BODY HAS OVER **600** SKELETAL MUSCLES.

SKELETAL?

SKELETAL MUSCLES CONTRACT TO PULL ON BONES OR OTHER TISSUES TO MOVE THEM. THEY CANNOT PUSH. THEY WORK IN PAIRS THAT PULL IN OPPOSITE DIRECTIONS.

WHAT DO OTHER MUSCLES DO?

SMOOTH MUSCLES MAKE THINGS MOVE INSIDE THE BODY, SUCH AS PUSHING FOOD THROUGH THE DIGESTIVE SYSTEM. SAYS HERE THEY'RE ALSO FOUND IN THE WALLS OF THE AIRWAYS AND BLOOD VESSELS.

AND ARE THERE ANY OTHER TYPES OF MUSCLES?

CARDIAC MUSCLES WORK DAY AND NIGHT TO KEEP THE HEART PUMPING—THAT'S THE MUSCLE MAKING ALL THOSE THUDDING SOUNDS! UNLIKE SKELETAL AND SMOOTH MUSCLES, CARDIAC MUSCLES ARE FOUND ONLY IN THE HEART!

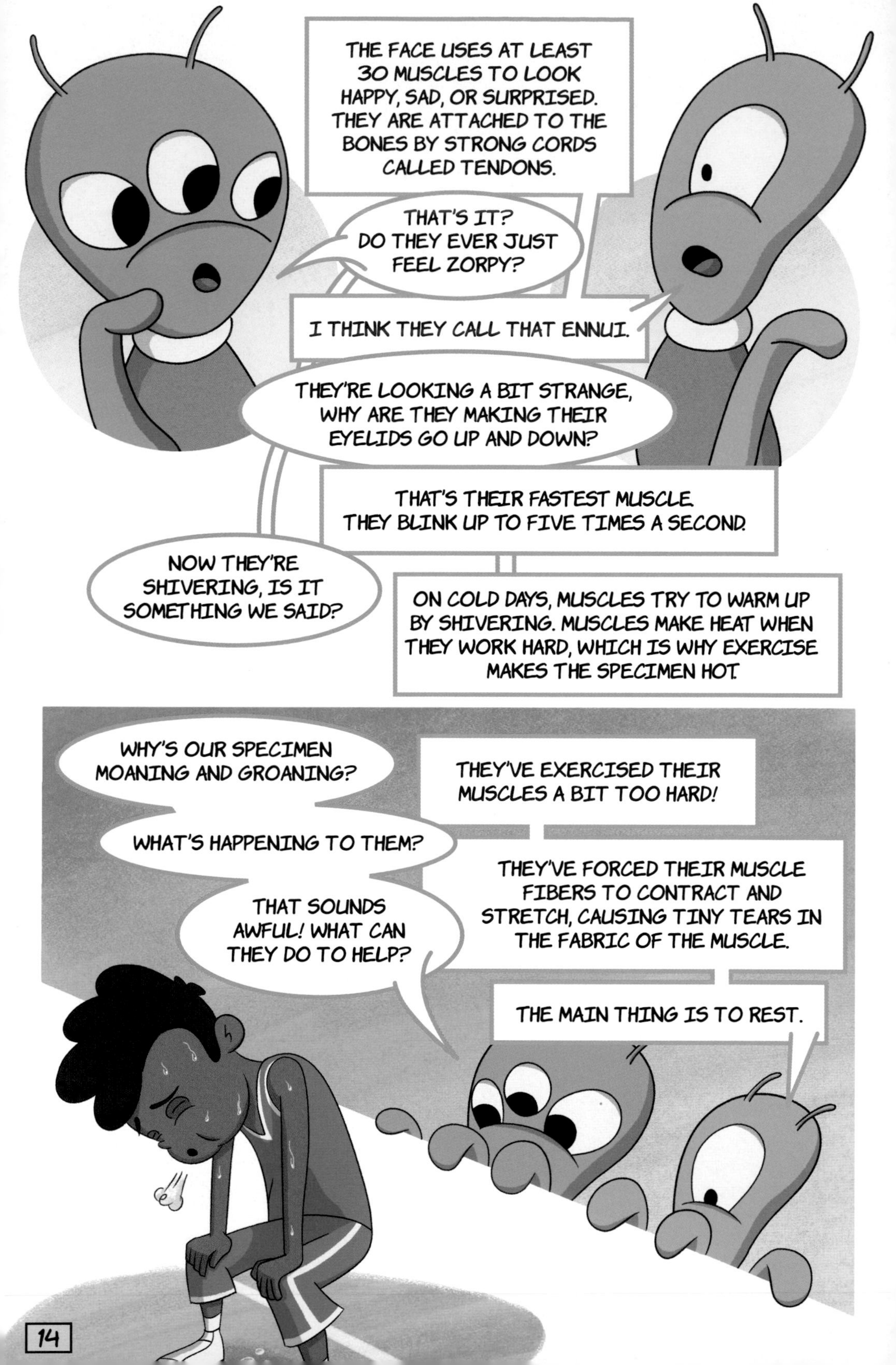
THE FACE USES AT LEAST 30 MUSCLES TO LOOK HAPPY, SAD, OR SURPRISED. THEY ARE ATTACHED TO THE BONES BY STRONG CORDS CALLED TENDONS.
THAT'S IT? DO THEY EVER JUST FEEL ZORPY?
I THINK THEY CALL THAT ENNUI.
THEY'RE LOOKING A BIT STRANGE, WHY ARE THEY MAKING THEIR EYELIDS GO UP AND DOWN?
THAT'S THEIR FASTEST MUSCLE. THEY BLINK UP TO FIVE TIMES A SECOND.
NOW THEY'RE SHIVERING, IS IT SOMETHING WE SAID?
ON COLD DAYS, MUSCLES TRY TO WARM UP BY SHIVERING. MUSCLES MAKE HEAT WHEN THEY WORK HARD, WHICH IS WHY EXERCISE MAKES THE SPECIMEN HOT.
WHY'S OUR SPECIMEN MOANING AND GROANING?
THEY'VE EXERCISED THEIR MUSCLES A BIT TOO HARD!
WHAT'S HAPPENING TO THEM?
THEY'VE FORCED THEIR MUSCLE FIBERS TO CONTRACT AND STRETCH, CAUSING TINY TEARS IN THE FABRIC OF THE MUSCLE.
THAT SOUNDS AWFUL! WHAT CAN THEY DO TO HELP?
THE MAIN THING IS TO REST.

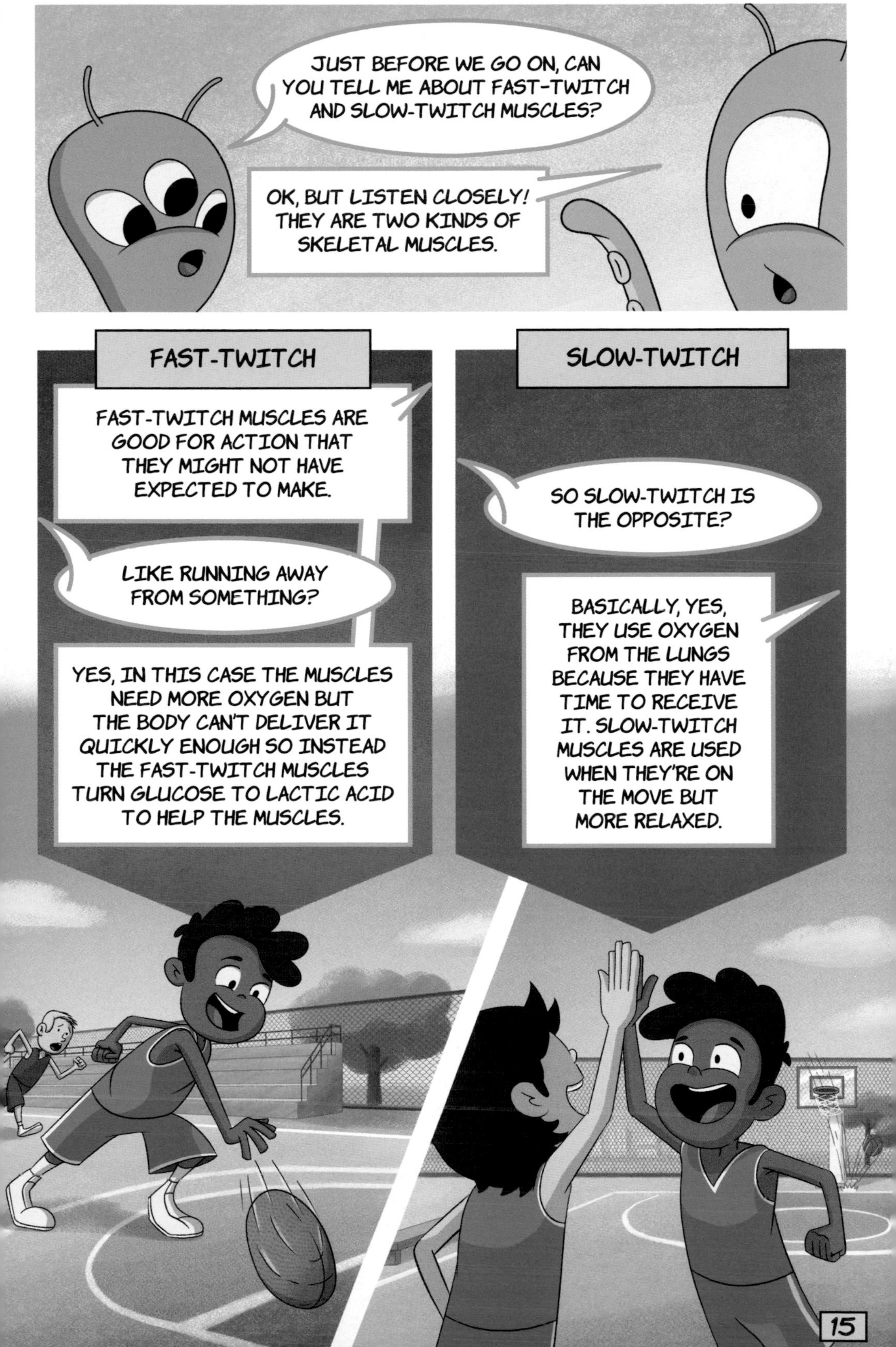
JUST BEFORE WE GO ON, CAN YOU TELL ME ABOUT FAST-TWITCH AND SLOW-TWITCH MUSCLES?
OK, BUT LISTEN CLOSELY! THEY ARE TWO KINDS OF SKELETAL MUSCLES.
FAST-TWITCH
FAST-TWITCH MUSCLES ARE GOOD FOR ACTION THAT THEY MIGHT NOT HAVE EXPECTED TO MAKE.
LIKE RUNNING AWAY FROM SOMETHING?
YES, IN THIS CASE THE MUSCLES NEED MORE OXYGEN BUT THE BODY CAN'T DELIVER IT QUICKLY ENOUGH SO INSTEAD THE FAST-TWITCH MUSCLES TURN GLUCOSE TO LACTIC ACID TO HELP THE MUSCLES.
SLOW-TWITCH
SO SLOW-TWITCH IS THE OPPOSITE?
BASICALLY, YES, THEY USE OXYGEN FROM THE LUNGS BECAUSE THEY HAVE TIME TO RECEIVE IT. SLOW-TWITCH MUSCLES ARE USED WHEN THEY'RE ON THE MOVE BUT MORE RELAXED.

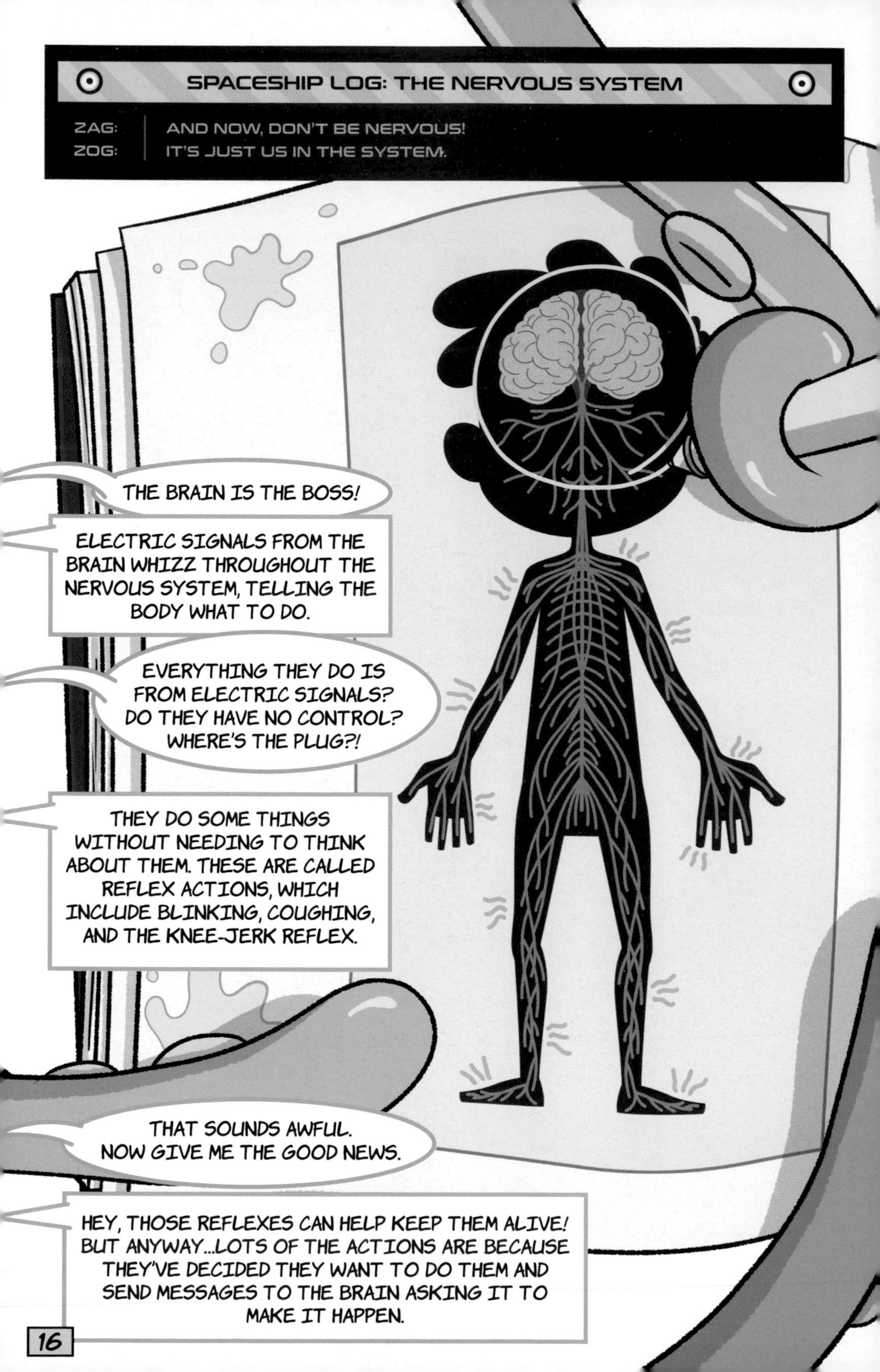
SPACESHIP LOG: THE NERVOUS SYSTEM
ZAG: AND NOW, DON'T BE NERVOUS!
ZOG: IT'S JUST US IN THE SYSTEM.
THE BRAIN IS THE BOSS!
ELECTRIC SIGNALS FROM THE BRAIN WHIZZ THROUGHOUT THE NERVOUS SYSTEM, TELLING THE BODY WHAT TO DO.
EVERYTHING THEY DO IS FROM ELECTRIC SIGNALS? DO THEY HAVE NO CONTROL? WHERE'S THE PLUG?!
THEY DO SOME THINGS WITHOUT NEEDING TO THINK ABOUT THEM. THESE ARE CALLED REFLEX ACTIONS, WHICH INCLUDE BLINKING, COUGHING, AND THE KNEE-JERK REFLEX.
THAT SOUNDS AWFUL. NOW GIVE ME THE GOOD NEWS.
HEY, THOSE REFLEXES CAN HELP KEEP THEM ALIVE! BUT ANYWAY...LOTS OF THE ACTIONS ARE BECAUSE THEY'VE DECIDED THEY WANT TO DO THEM AND SEND MESSAGES TO THE BRAIN ASKING IT TO MAKE IT HAPPEN.

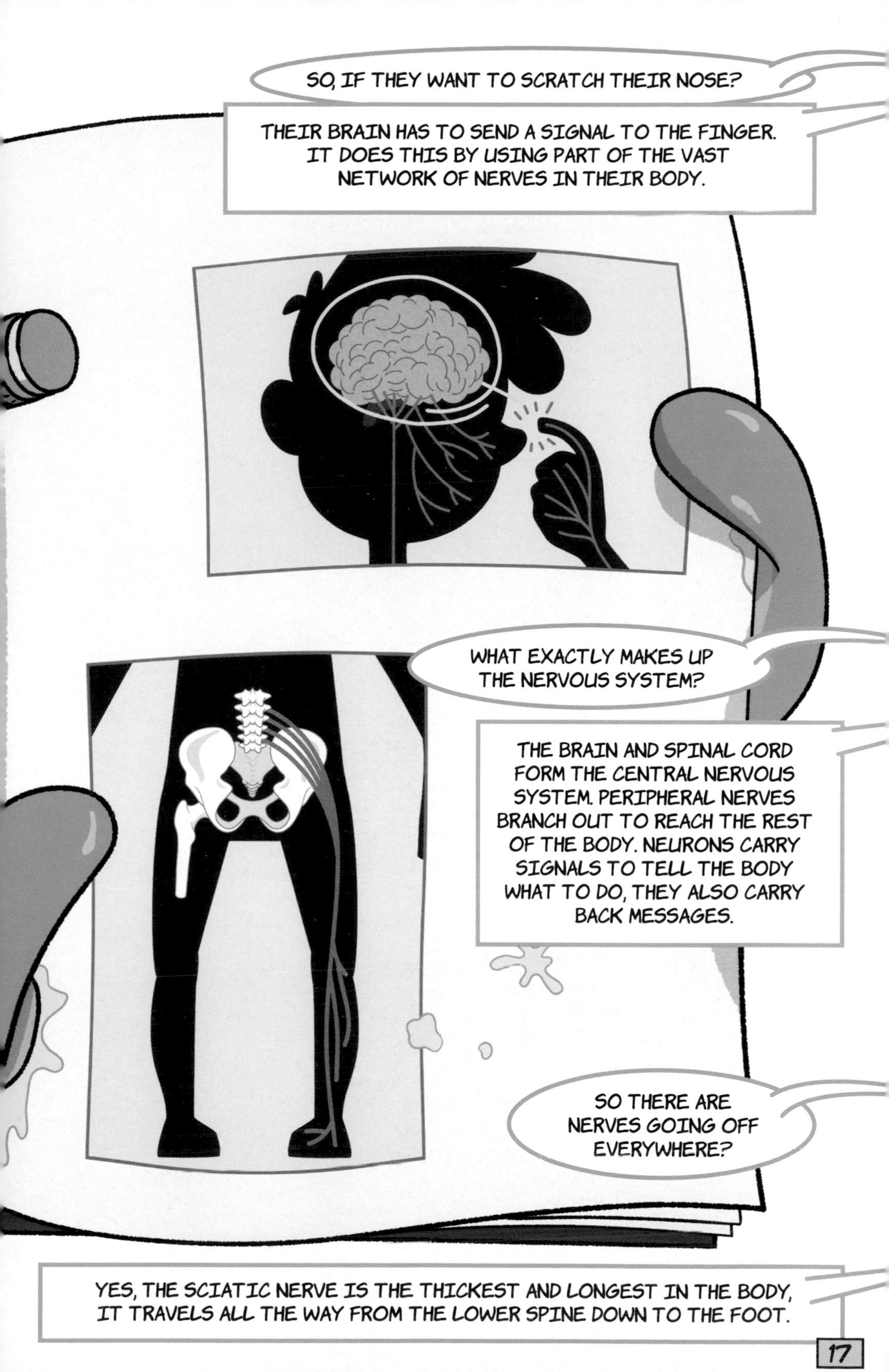

SO, IF THEY WANT TO SCRATCH THEIR NOSE?
THEIR BRAIN HAS TO SEND A SIGNAL TO THE FINGER. IT DOES THIS BY USING PART OF THE VAST NETWORK OF NERVES IN THEIR BODY.
WHAT EXACTLY MAKES UP THE NERVOUS SYSTEM?
THE BRAIN AND SPINAL CORD FORM THE CENTRAL NERVOUS SYSTEM. PERIPHERAL NERVES BRANCH OUT TO REACH THE REST OF THE BODY. NEURONS CARRY SIGNALS TO TELL THE BODY WHAT TO DO, THEY ALSO CARRY BACK MESSAGES.
SO THERE ARE NERVES GOING OFF EVERYWHERE?
YES, THE SCIATIC NERVE IS THE THICKEST AND LONGEST IN THE BODY, IT TRAVELS ALL THE WAY FROM THE LOWER SPINE DOWN TO THE FOOT.

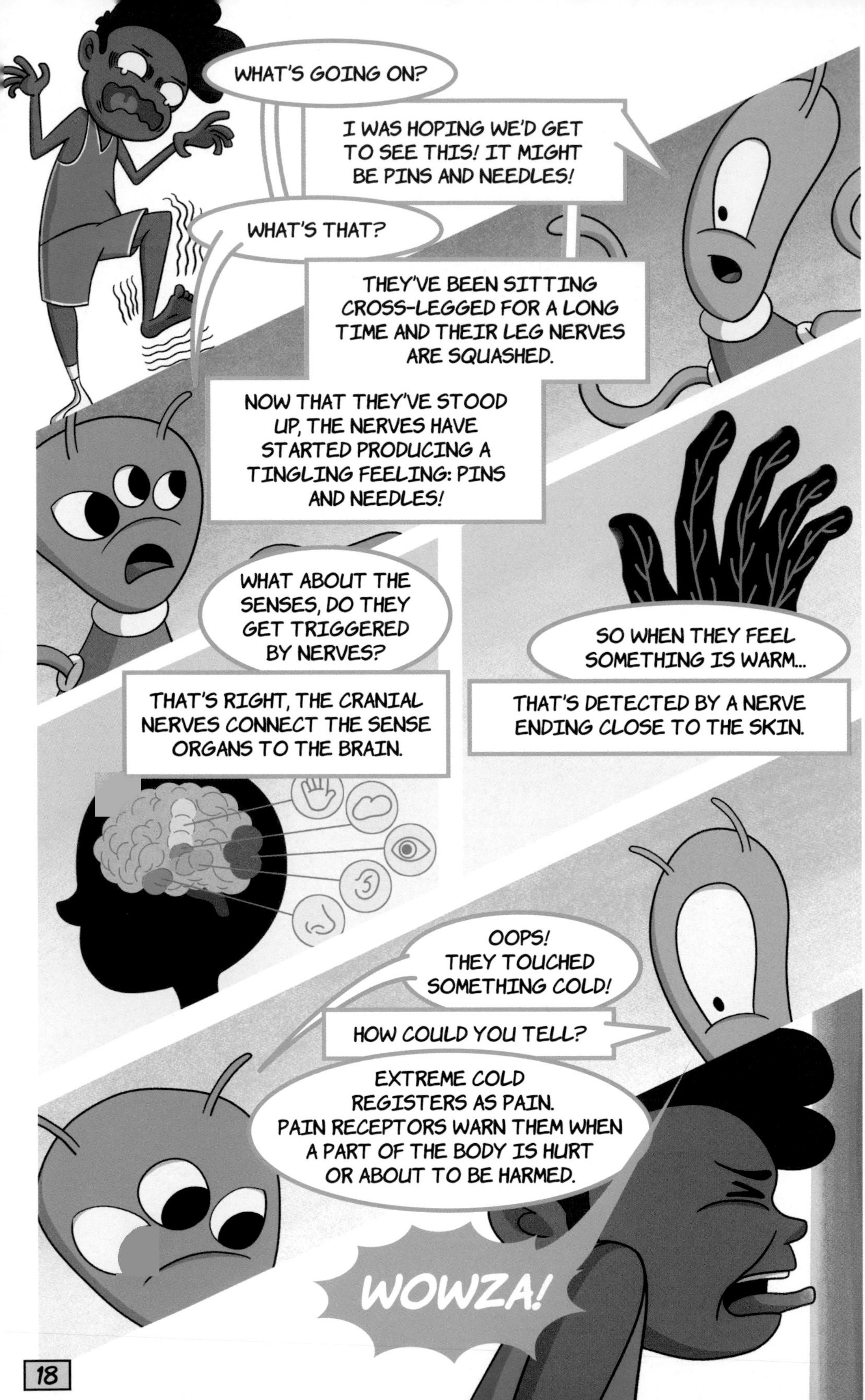
WHAT'S GOING ON?
I WAS HOPING WE'D GET TO SEE THIS! IT MIGHT BE PINS AND NEEDLES!
WHAT'S THAT?
THEY'VE BEEN SITTING CROSS-LEGGED FOR A LONG TIME AND THEIR LEG NERVES ARE SQUASHED.
NOW THAT THEY'VE STOOD UP, THE NERVES HAVE STARTED PRODUCING A TINGLING FEELING: PINS AND NEEDLES!
WHAT ABOUT THE SENSES, DO THEY GET TRIGGERED BY NERVES?
THAT'S RIGHT, THE CRANIAL NERVES CONNECT THE SENSE ORGANS TO THE BRAIN.
SO WHEN THEY FEEL SOMETHING IS WARM...
THAT'S DETECTED BY A NERVE ENDING CLOSE TO THE SKIN.
OOPS! THEY TOUCHED SOMETHING COLD!
HOW COULD YOU TELL?
EXTREME COLD REGISTERS AS PAIN. PAIN RECEPTORS WARN THEM WHEN A PART OF THE BODY IS HURT OR ABOUT TO BE HARMED.
WOWZA!

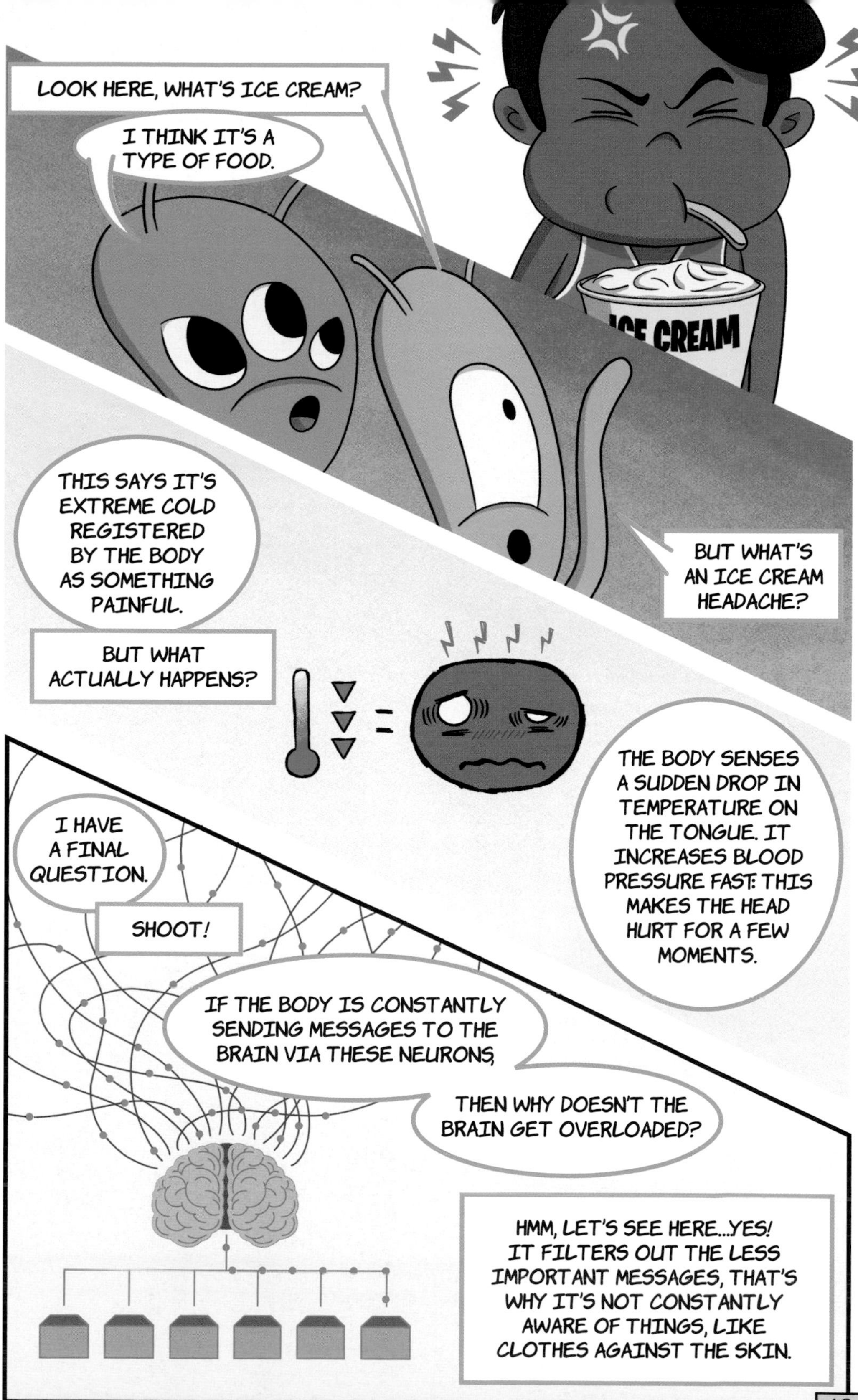
LOOK HERE, WHAT'S ICE CREAM?
I THINK IT'S A TYPE OF FOOD.
ICE CREAM
THIS SAYS IT'S EXTREME COLD REGISTERED BY THE BODY AS SOMETHING PAINFUL.
BUT WHAT'S AN ICE CREAM HEADACHE?
BUT WHAT ACTUALLY HAPPENS?
THE BODY SENSES A SUDDEN DROP IN TEMPERATURE ON THE TONGUE. IT INCREASES BLOOD PRESSURE FAST: THIS MAKES THE HEAD HURT FOR A FEW MOMENTS.
I HAVE A FINAL QUESTION.
SHOOT!
IF THE BODY IS CONSTANTLY SENDING MESSAGES TO THE BRAIN VIA THESE NEURONS,
THEN WHY DOESN'T THE BRAIN GET OVERLOADED?
HMM, LET'S SEE HERE...YES! IT FILTERS OUT THE LESS IMPORTANT MESSAGES, THAT'S WHY IT'S NOT CONSTANTLY AWARE OF THINGS, LIKE CLOTHES AGAINST THE SKIN.

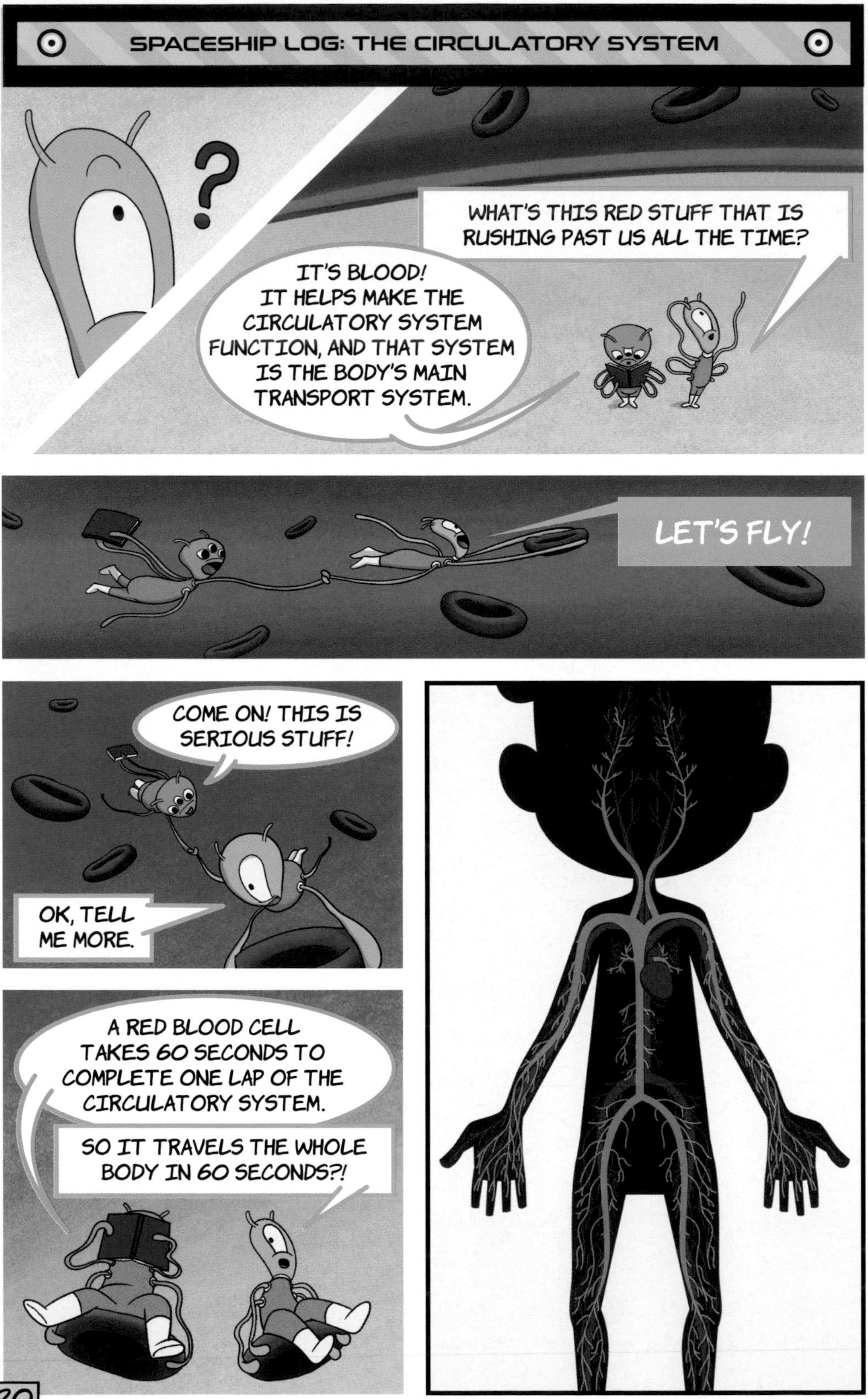
SPACESHIP LOG: THE CIRCULATORY SYSTEM
?
WHAT'S THIS RED STUFF THAT IS RUSHING PAST US ALL THE TIME?
IT'S BLOOD! IT HELPS MAKE THE CIRCULATORY SYSTEM FUNCTION, AND THAT SYSTEM IS THE BODY'S MAIN TRANSPORT SYSTEM.
LET'S FLY!
COME ON! THIS IS SERIOUS STUFF!
OK, TELL ME MORE.
A RED BLOOD CELL TAKES 60 SECONDS TO COMPLETE ONE LAP OF THE CIRCULATORY SYSTEM.
SO IT TRAVELS THE WHOLE BODY IN 60 SECONDS?!

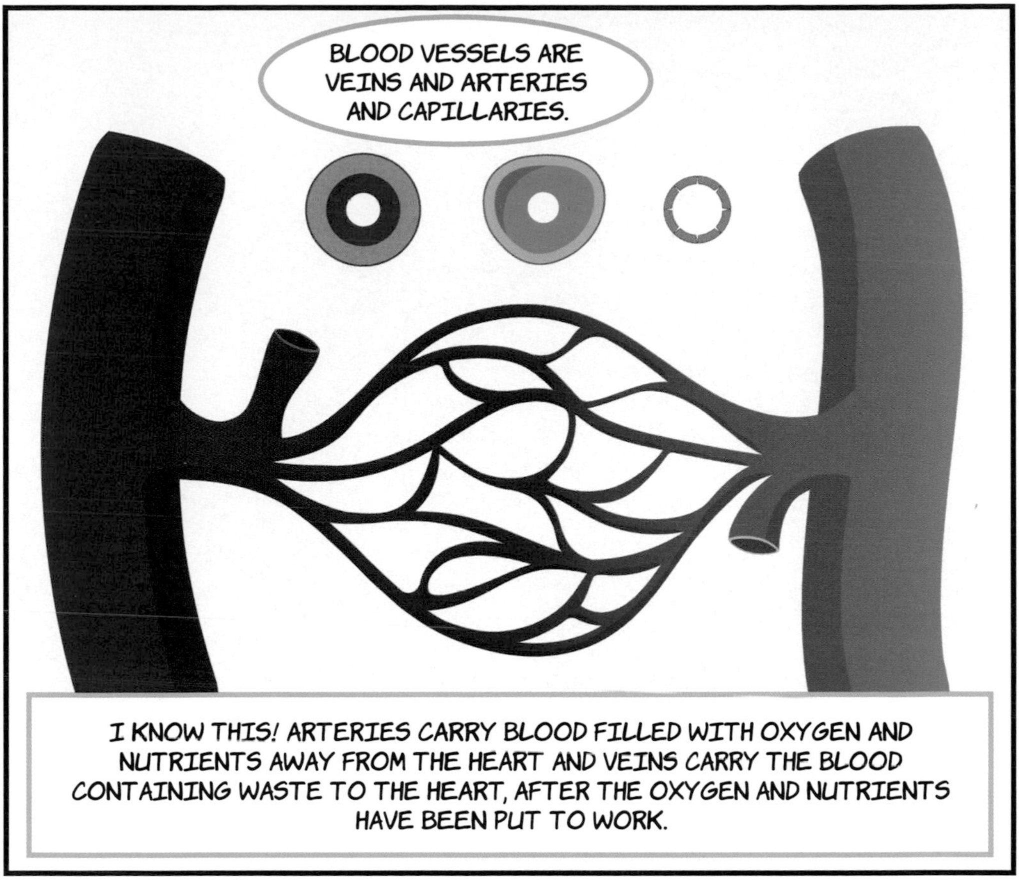
BLOOD VESSELS ARE VEINS AND ARTERIES AND CAPILLARIES.
I KNOW THIS! ARTERIES CARRY BLOOD FILLED WITH OXYGEN AND NUTRIENTS AWAY FROM THE HEART AND VEINS CARRY THE BLOOD CONTAINING WASTE TO THE HEART, AFTER THE OXYGEN AND NUTRIENTS HAVE BEEN PUT TO WORK.

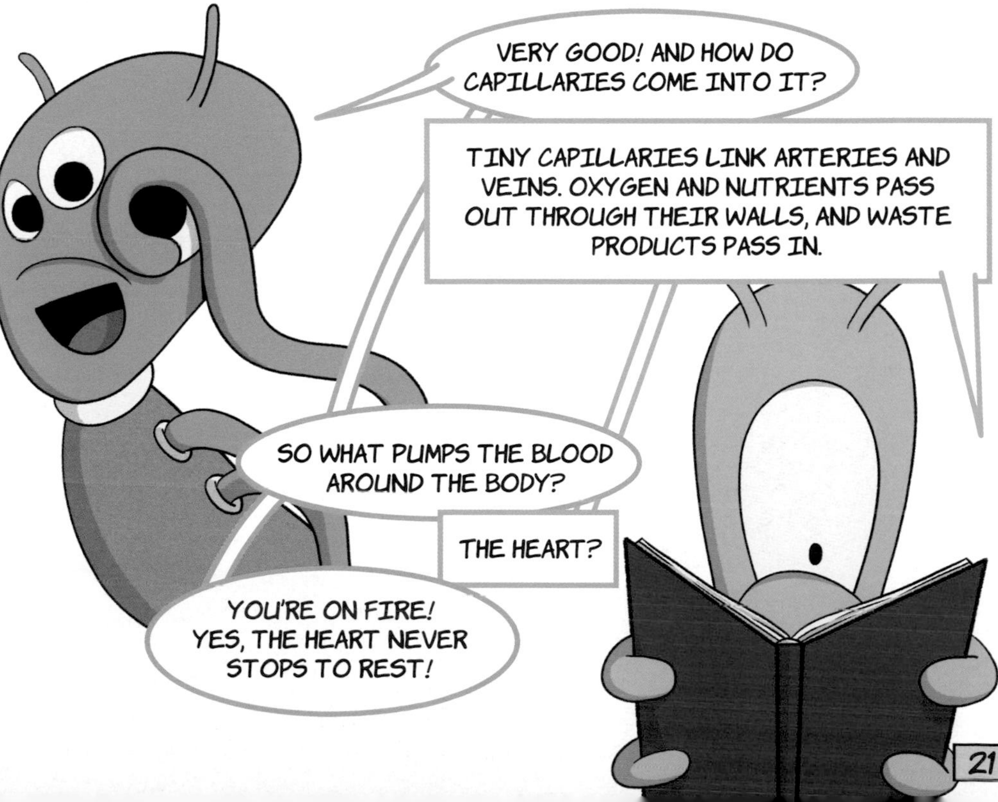
VERY GOOD! AND HOW DO CAPILLARIES COME INTO IT?
TINY CAPILLARIES LINK ARTERIES AND VEINS. OXYGEN AND NUTRIENTS PASS OUT THROUGH THEIR WALLS, AND WASTE PRODUCTS PASS IN.
SO WHAT PUMPS THE BLOOD AROUND THE BODY?
THE HEART?
YOU'RE ON FIRE! YES, THE HEART NEVER STOPS TO REST!

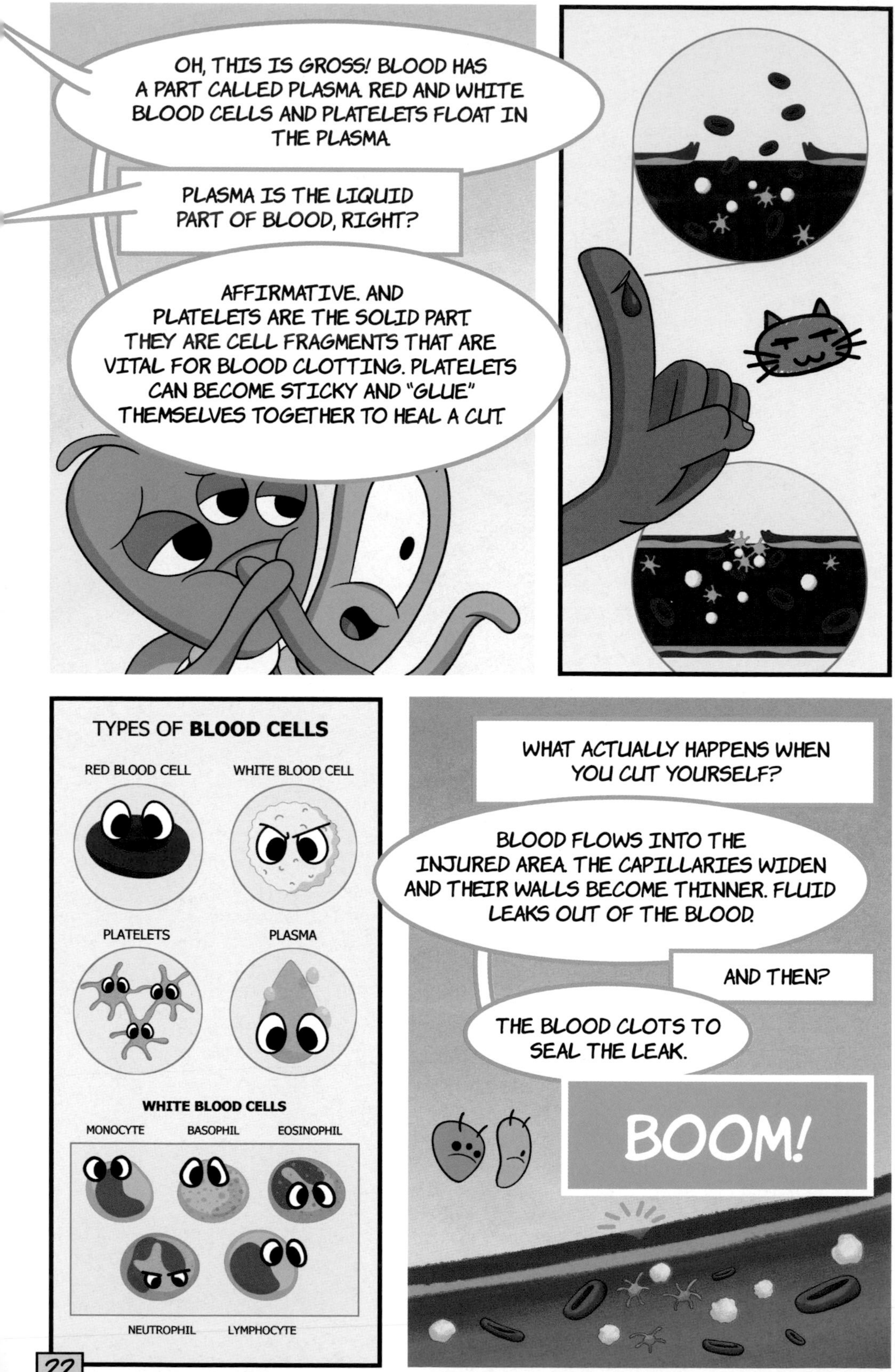
OH, THIS IS GROSS! BLOOD HAS A PART CALLED PLASMA. RED AND WHITE BLOOD CELLS AND PLATELETS FLOAT IN THE PLASMA.
PLASMA IS THE LIQUID PART OF BLOOD, RIGHT?
AFFIRMATIVE. AND PLATELETS ARE THE SOLID PART. THEY ARE CELL FRAGMENTS THAT ARE VITAL FOR BLOOD CLOTTING. PLATELETS CAN BECOME STICKY AND "GLUE" THEMSELVES TOGETHER TO HEAL A CUT.
TYPES OF BLOOD CELLS
RED BLOOD CELL
WHITE BLOOD CELL
PLATELETS
PLASMA
WHITE BLOOD CELLS
MONOCYTE
BASOPHIL
EOSINOPHIL
NEUTROPHIL
LYMPHOCYTE
WHAT ACTUALLY HAPPENS WHEN YOU CUT YOURSELF?
BLOOD FLOWS INTO THE INJURED AREA. THE CAPILLARIES WIDEN AND THEIR WALLS BECOME THINNER. FLUID LEAKS OUT OF THE BLOOD.
AND THEN?
THE BLOOD CLOTS TO SEAL THE LEAK.
BOOM!

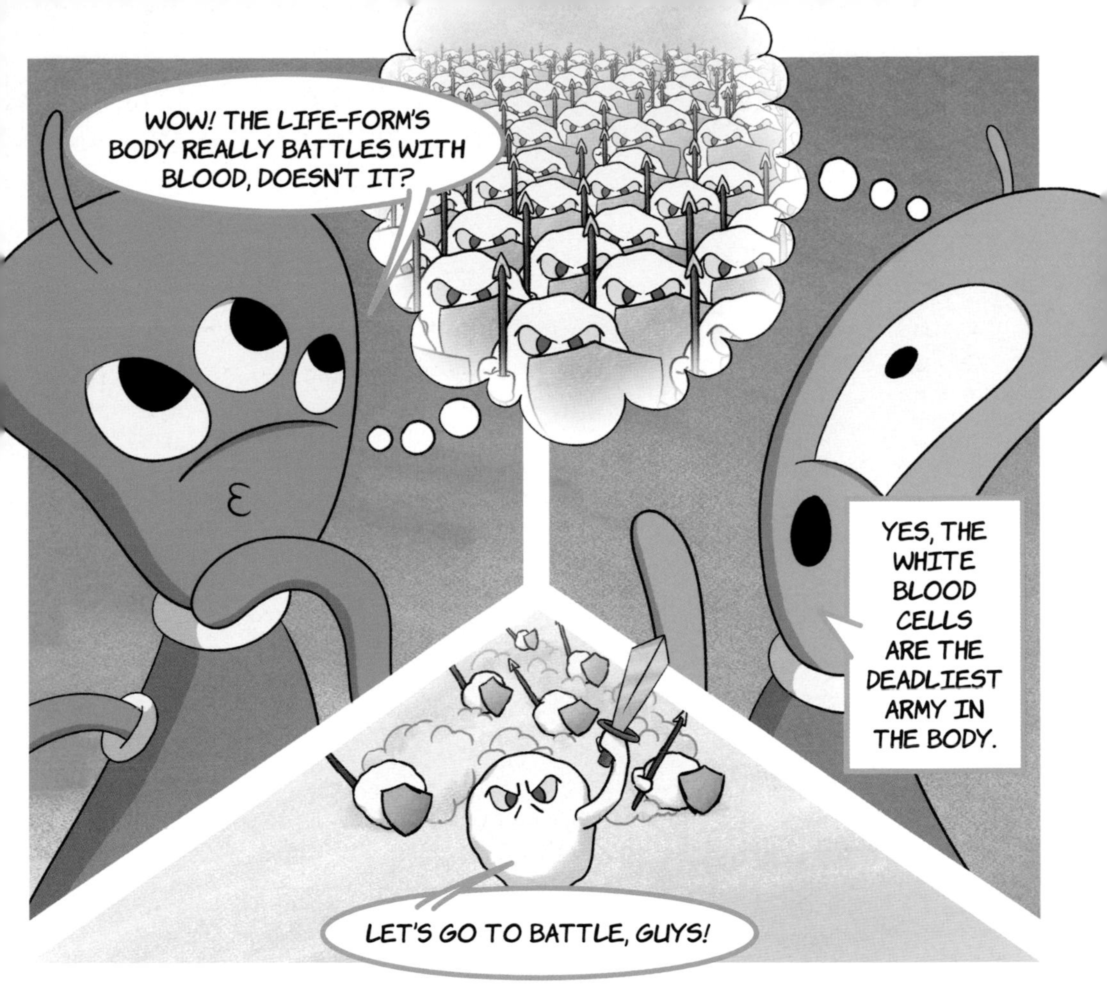
WOW! THE LIFE-FORM'S BODY REALLY BATTLES WITH BLOOD, DOESN'T IT?
YES, THE WHITE BLOOD CELLS ARE THE DEADLIEST ARMY IN THE BODY.
LET'S GO TO BATTLE, GUYS!

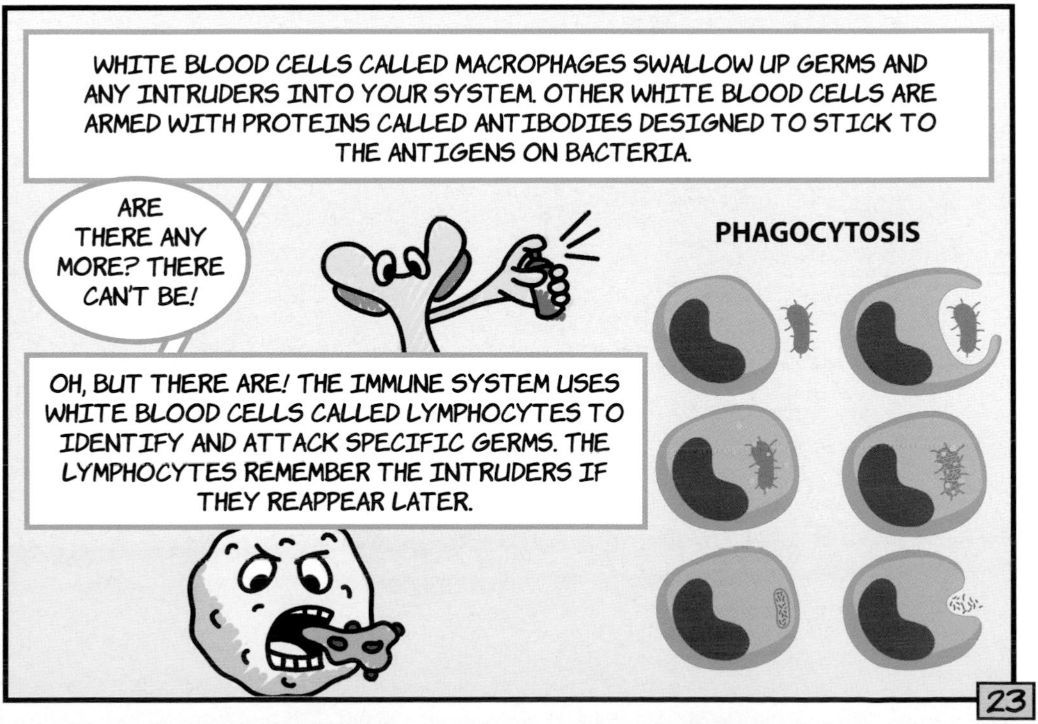
WHITE BLOOD CELLS CALLED MACROPHAGES SWALLOW UP GERMS AND ANY INTRUDERS INTO YOUR SYSTEM. OTHER WHITE BLOOD CELLS ARE ARMED WITH PROTEINS CALLED ANTIBODIES DESIGNED TO STICK TO THE ANTIGENS ON BACTERIA.
ARE THERE ANY MORE? THERE CAN'T BE!
PHAGOCYTOSIS
OH, BUT THERE ARE! THE IMMUNE SYSTEM USES WHITE BLOOD CELLS CALLED LYMPHOCYTES TO IDENTIFY AND ATTACK SPECIFIC GERMS. THE LYMPHOCYTES REMEMBER THE INTRUDERS IF THEY REAPPEAR LATER.

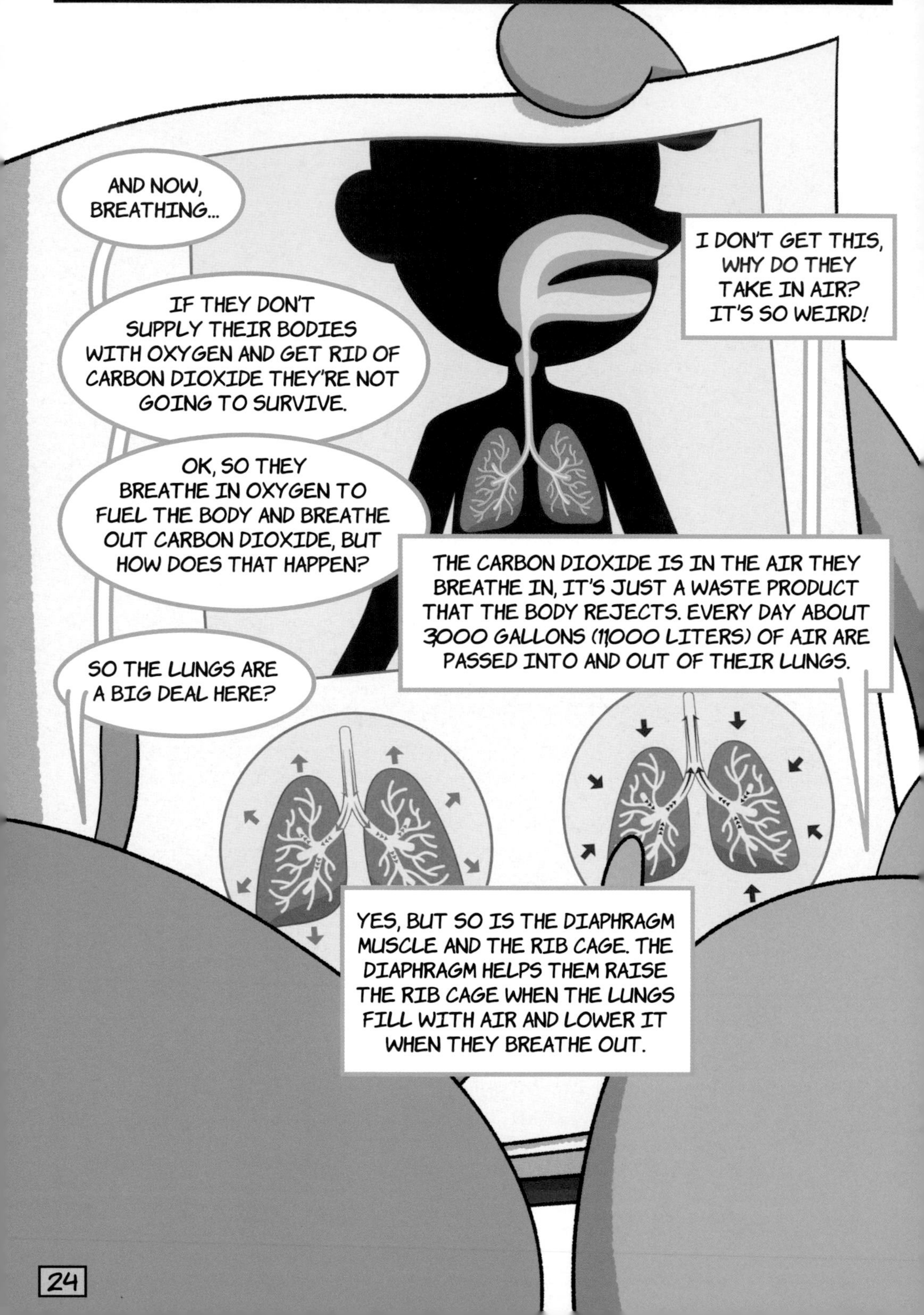
AND NOW, BREATHING...
IF THEY DON'T SUPPLY THEIR BODIES WITH OXYGEN AND GET RID OF CARBON DIOXIDE THEY'RE NOT GOING TO SURVIVE.
I DON'T GET THIS, WHY DO THEY TAKE IN AIR? IT'S SO WEIRD!
OK, SO THEY BREATHE IN OXYGEN TO FUEL THE BODY AND BREATHE OUT CARBON DIOXIDE, BUT HOW DOES THAT HAPPEN?
THE CARBON DIOXIDE IS IN THE AIR THEY BREATHE IN, IT'S JUST A WASTE PRODUCT THAT THE BODY REJECTS. EVERY DAY ABOUT 3000 GALLONS (11000 LITERS) OF AIR ARE PASSED INTO AND OUT OF THEIR LUNGS.
SO THE LUNGS ARE A BIG DEAL HERE?
YES, BUT SO IS THE DIAPHRAGM MUSCLE AND THE RIB CAGE. THE DIAPHRAGM HELPS THEM RAISE THE RIB CAGE WHEN THE LUNGS FILL WITH AIR AND LOWER IT WHEN THEY BREATHE OUT.

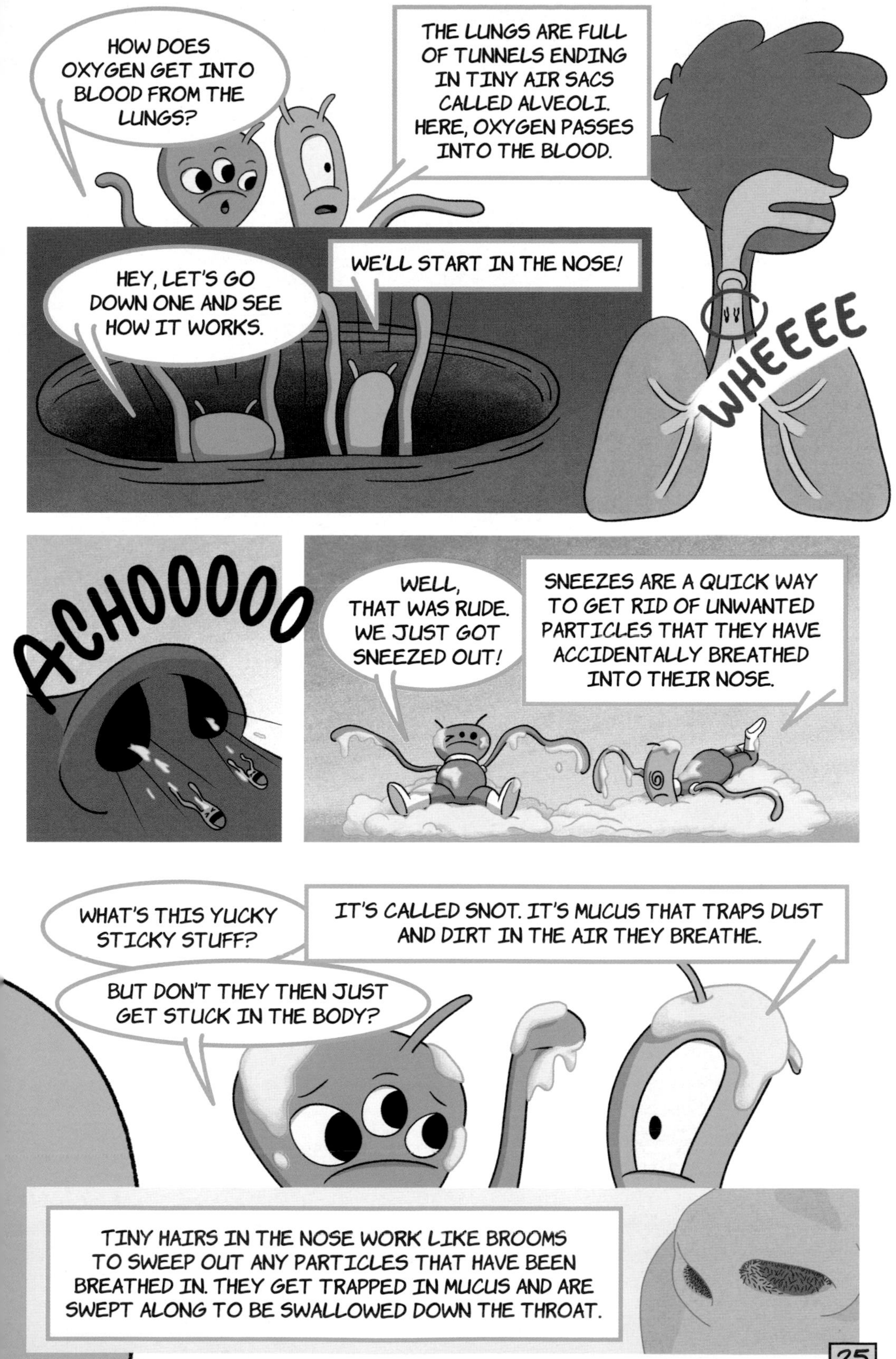
HOW DOES OXYGEN GET INTO BLOOD FROM THE LUNGS?
THE LUNGS ARE FULL OF TUNNELS ENDING IN TINY AIR SACS CALLED ALVEOLI. HERE, OXYGEN PASSES INTO THE BLOOD.
HEY, LET'S GO DOWN ONE AND SEE HOW IT WORKS.
WE'LL START IN THE NOSE!
WHEEEE
ACHOOOOO
WELL, THAT WAS RUDE. WE JUST GOT SNEEZED OUT!
SNEEZES ARE A QUICK WAY TO GET RID OF UNWANTED PARTICLES THAT THEY HAVE ACCIDENTALLY BREATHED INTO THEIR NOSE.
WHAT'S THIS YUCKY STICKY STUFF?
IT'S CALLED SNOT. IT'S MUCUS THAT TRAPS DUST AND DIRT IN THE AIR THEY BREATHE.
BUT DON'T THEY THEN JUST GET STUCK IN THE BODY?
TINY HAIRS IN THE NOSE WORK LIKE BROOMS TO SWEEP OUT ANY PARTICLES THAT HAVE BEEN BREATHED IN. THEY GET TRAPPED IN MUCUS AND ARE SWEPT ALONG TO BE SWALLOWED DOWN THE THROAT.

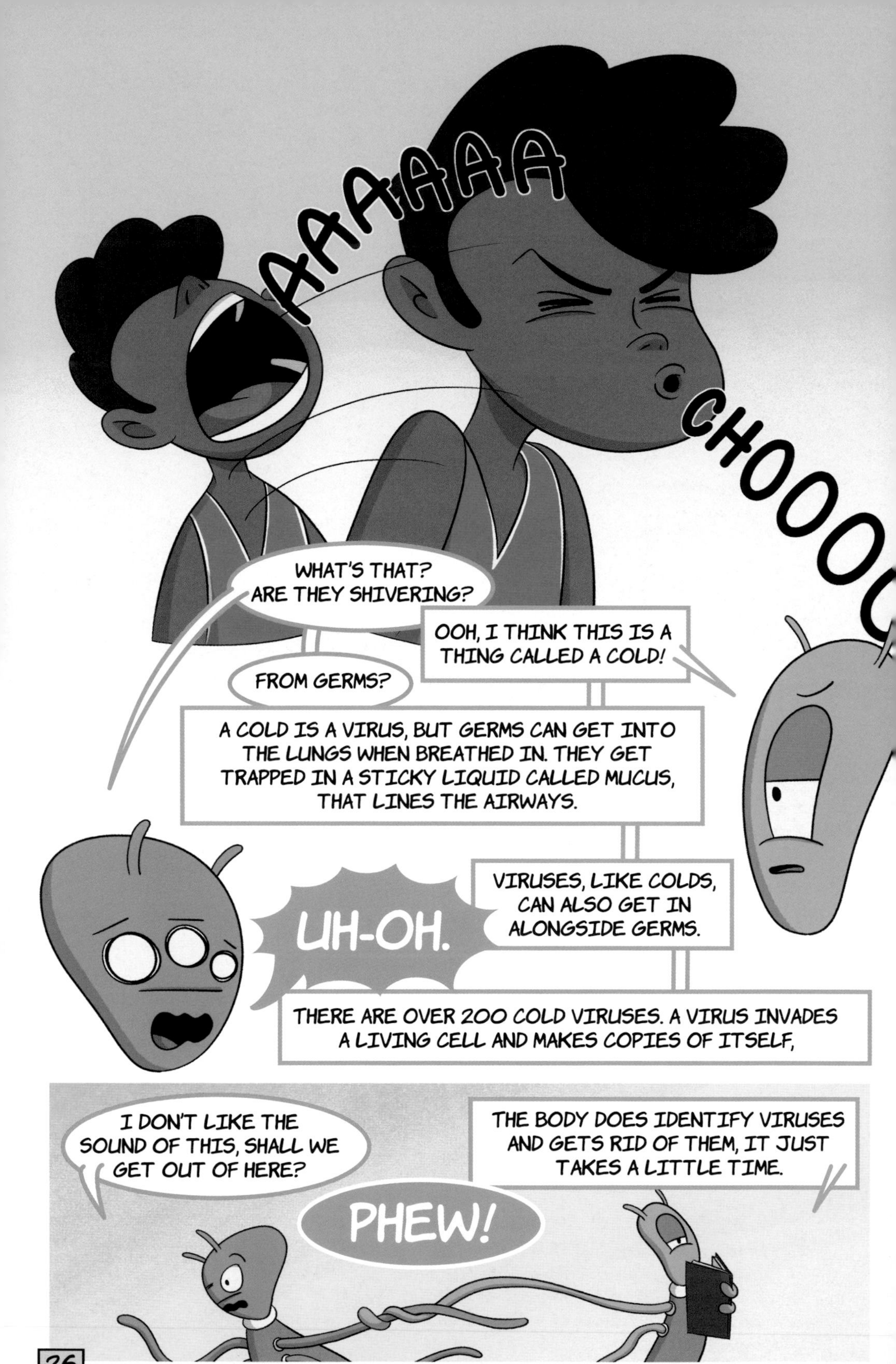

AAAAAA
CHOOOO
WHAT'S THAT? ARE THEY SHIVERING?
OOH, I THINK THIS IS A THING CALLED A COLD!
FROM GERMS?
A COLD IS A VIRUS, BUT GERMS CAN GET INTO THE LUNGS WHEN BREATHED IN. THEY GET TRAPPED IN A STICKY LIQUID CALLED MUCUS, THAT LINES THE AIRWAYS.
UH-OH.
VIRUSES, LIKE COLDS, CAN ALSO GET IN ALONGSIDE GERMS.
THERE ARE OVER 200 COLD VIRUSES. A VIRUS INVADES A LIVING CELL AND MAKES COPIES OF ITSELF,
I DON'T LIKE THE SOUND OF THIS, SHALL WE GET OUT OF HERE?
THE BODY DOES IDENTIFY VIRUSES AND GETS RID OF THEM, IT JUST TAKES A LITTLE TIME.
PHEW!

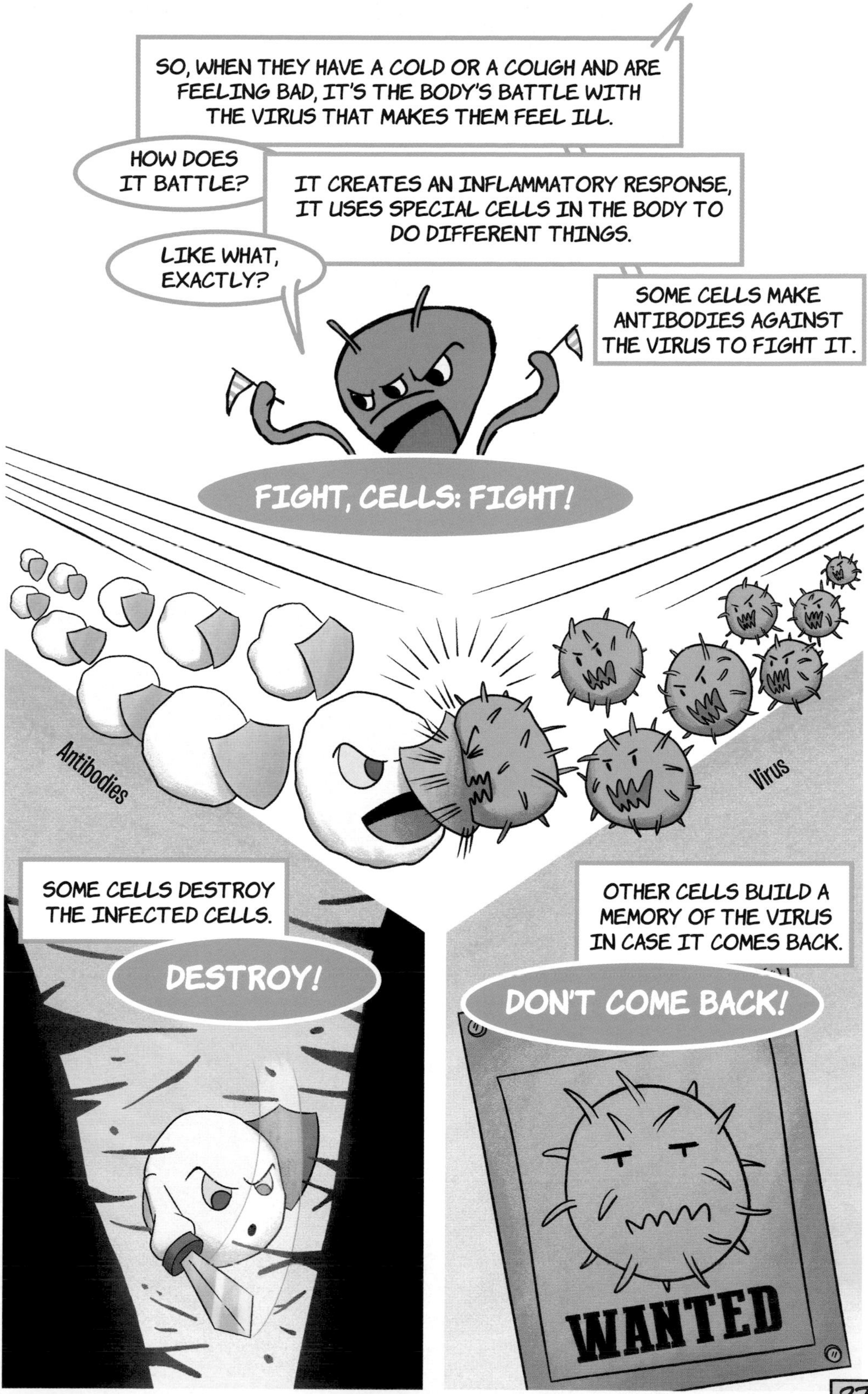
SO, WHEN THEY HAVE A COLD OR A COUGH AND ARE FEELING BAD, IT'S THE BODY'S BATTLE WITH THE VIRUS THAT MAKES THEM FEEL ILL.
HOW DOES IT BATTLE?
IT CREATES AN INFLAMMATORY RESPONSE, IT USES SPECIAL CELLS IN THE BODY TO DO DIFFERENT THINGS.
LIKE WHAT, EXACTLY?
SOME CELLS MAKE ANTIBODIES AGAINST THE VIRUS TO FIGHT IT.
FIGHT, CELLS: FIGHT!
Antibodies
Virus
SOME CELLS DESTROY THE INFECTED CELLS.
DESTROY!
OTHER CELLS BUILD A MEMORY OF THE VIRUS IN CASE IT COMES BACK.
DON'T COME BACK!
WANTED

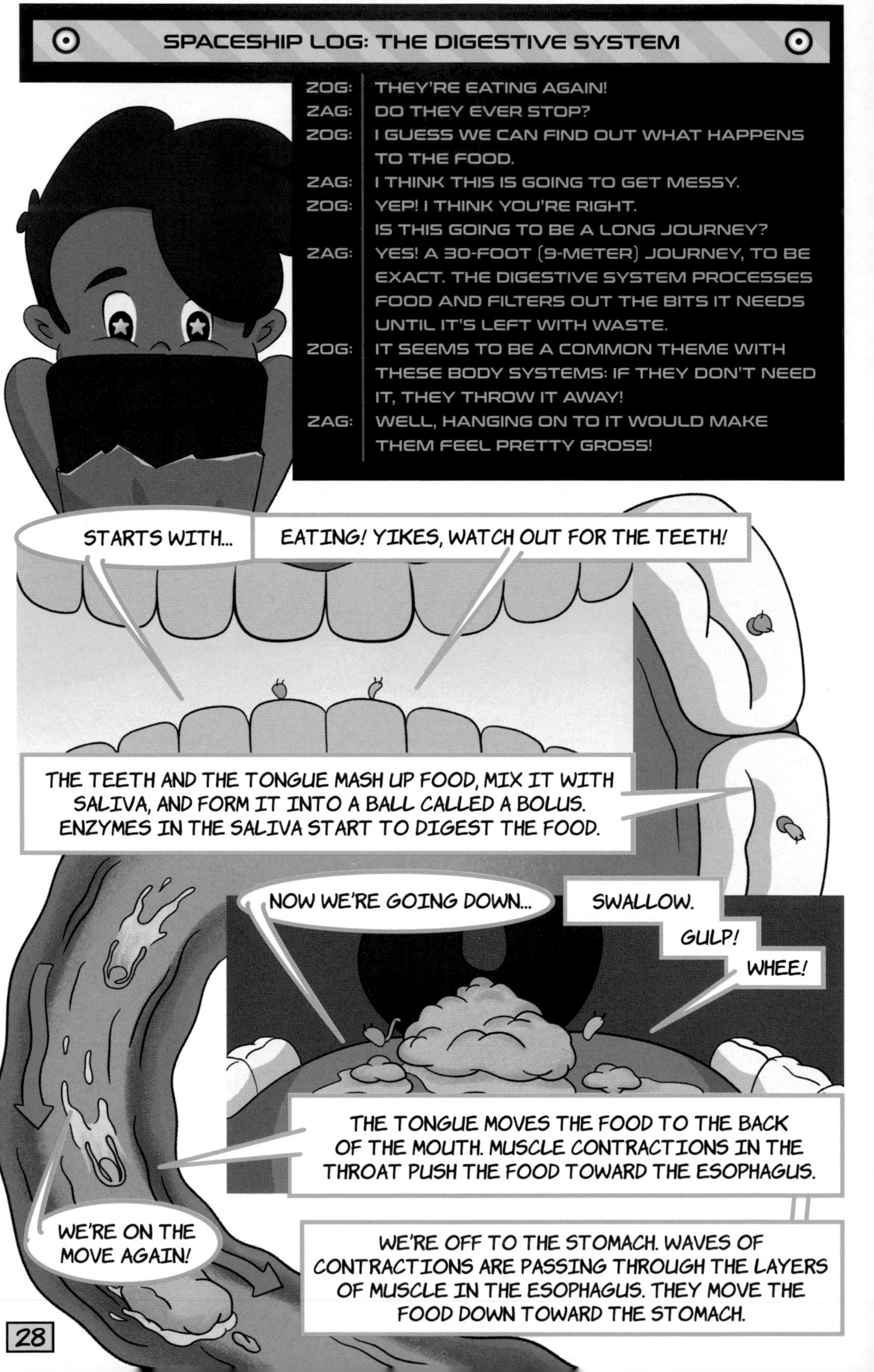
SPACESHIP LOG: THE DIGESTIVE SYSTEM
ZOG: THEY'RE EATING AGAIN!
ZAG: DO THEY EVER STOP?
ZOG: I GUESS WE CAN FIND OUT WHAT HAPPENS TO THE FOOD.
ZAG: I THINK THIS IS GOING TO GET MESSY.
ZOG: YEP! I THINK YOU'RE RIGHT. IS THIS GOING TO BE A LONG JOURNEY?
ZAG: YES! A 30-FOOT (9-METER) JOURNEY, TO BE EXACT. THE DIGESTIVE SYSTEM PROCESSES FOOD AND FILTERS OUT THE BITS IT NEEDS UNTIL IT'S LEFT WITH WASTE.
ZOG: IT SEEMS TO BE A COMMON THEME WITH THESE BODY SYSTEMS: IF THEY DON'T NEED IT, THEY THROW IT AWAY!
ZAG: WELL, HANGING ON TO IT WOULD MAKE THEM FEEL PRETTY GROSS!
STARTS WITH...
EATING! YIKES, WATCH OUT FOR THE TEETH!
THE TEETH AND THE TONGUE MASH UP FOOD, MIX IT WITH SALIVA, AND FORM IT INTO A BALL CALLED A BOLUS. ENZYMES IN THE SALIVA START TO DIGEST THE FOOD.
NOW WE'RE GOING DOWN...
SWALLOW.
GULP!
WHEE!
THE TONGUE MOVES THE FOOD TO THE BACK OF THE MOUTH. MUSCLE CONTRACTIONS IN THE THROAT PUSH THE FOOD TOWARD THE ESOPHAGUS.
WE'RE ON THE MOVE AGAIN!
WE'RE OFF TO THE STOMACH. WAVES OF CONTRACTIONS ARE PASSING THROUGH THE LAYERS OF MUSCLE IN THE ESOPHAGUS. THEY MOVE THE FOOD DOWN TOWARD THE STOMACH.

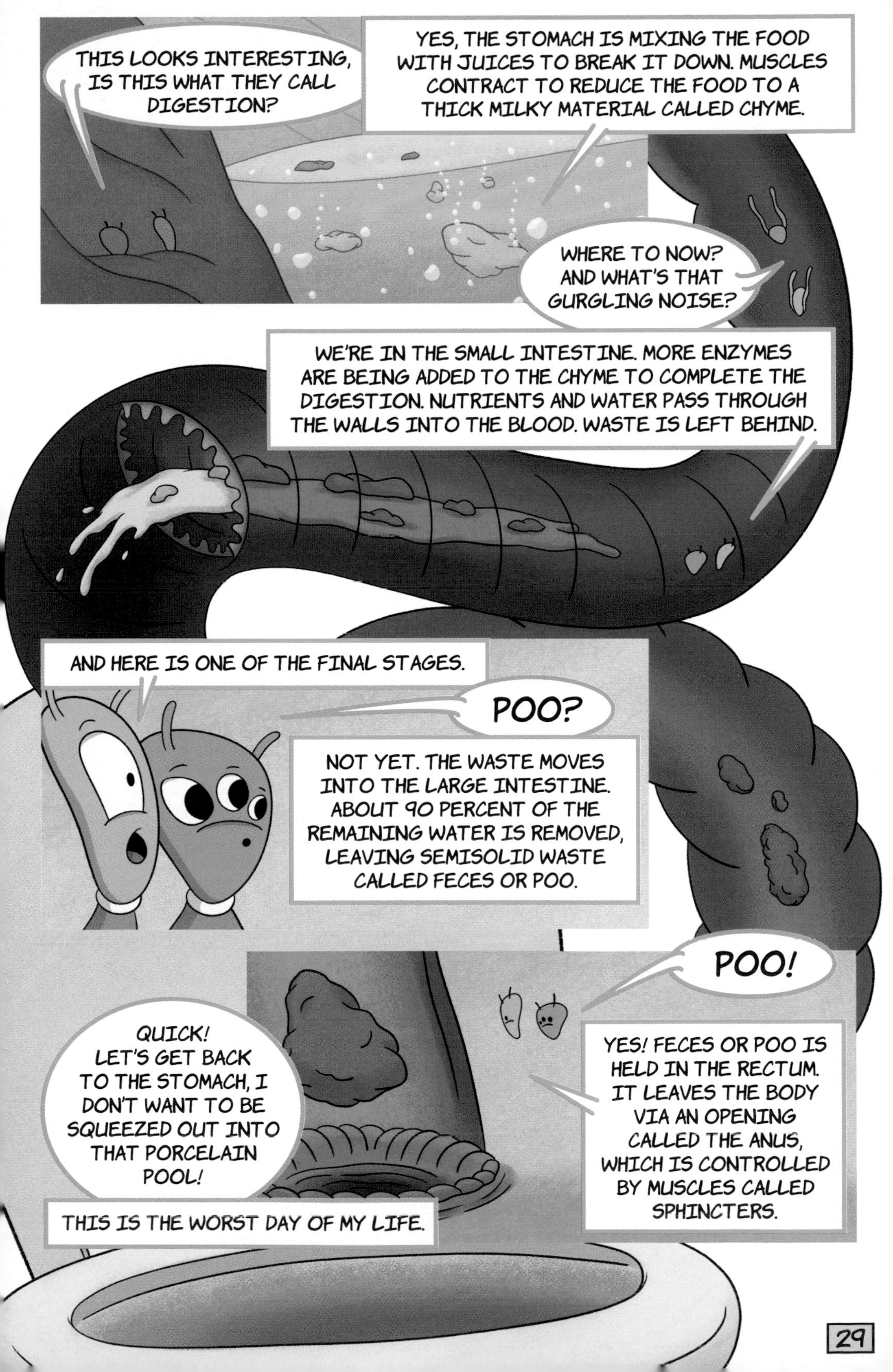
THIS LOOKS INTERESTING, IS THIS WHAT THEY CALL DIGESTION?
YES, THE STOMACH IS MIXING THE FOOD WITH JUICES TO BREAK IT DOWN. MUSCLES CONTRACT TO REDUCE THE FOOD TO A THICK MILKY MATERIAL CALLED CHYME.
WHERE TO NOW? AND WHAT'S THAT GURGLING NOISE?
WE'RE IN THE SMALL INTESTINE. MORE ENZYMES ARE BEING ADDED TO THE CHYME TO COMPLETE THE DIGESTION. NUTRIENTS AND WATER PASS THROUGH THE WALLS INTO THE BLOOD. WASTE IS LEFT BEHIND.
AND HERE IS ONE OF THE FINAL STAGES.
POO?
NOT YET. THE WASTE MOVES INTO THE LARGE INTESTINE. ABOUT 90 PERCENT OF THE REMAINING WATER IS REMOVED, LEAVING SEMISOLID WASTE CALLED FECES OR POO.
POO!
YES! FECES OR POO IS HELD IN THE RECTUM. IT LEAVES THE BODY VIA AN OPENING CALLED THE ANUS, WHICH IS CONTROLLED BY MUSCLES CALLED SPHINCTERS.
QUICK! LET'S GET BACK TO THE STOMACH, I DON'T WANT TO BE SQUEEZED OUT INTO THAT PORCELAIN POOL!
THIS IS THE WORST DAY OF MY LIFE.

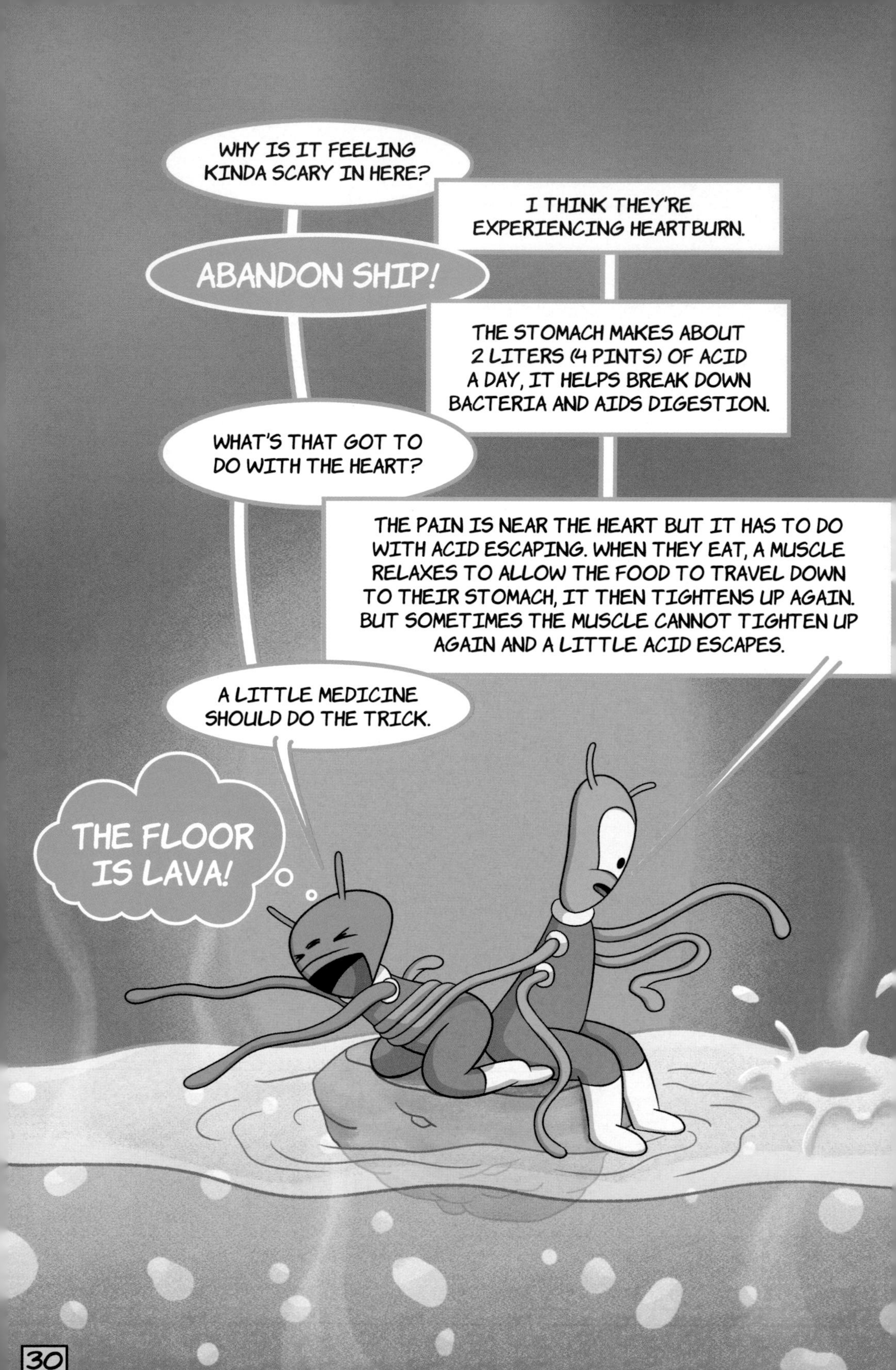
WHY IS IT FEELING KINDA SCARY IN HERE?
I THINK THEY'RE EXPERIENCING HEARTBURN.
ABANDON SHIP!
THE STOMACH MAKES ABOUT 2 LITERS (4 PINTS) OF ACID A DAY, IT HELPS BREAK DOWN BACTERIA AND AIDS DIGESTION.
WHAT'S THAT GOT TO DO WITH THE HEART?
THE PAIN IS NEAR THE HEART BUT IT HAS TO DO WITH ACID ESCAPING. WHEN THEY EAT, A MUSCLE RELAXES TO ALLOW THE FOOD TO TRAVEL DOWN TO THEIR STOMACH, IT THEN TIGHTENS UP AGAIN. BUT SOMETIMES THE MUSCLE CANNOT TIGHTEN UP AGAIN AND A LITTLE ACID ESCAPES.
A LITTLE MEDICINE SHOULD DO THE TRICK.
THE FLOOR IS LAVA!

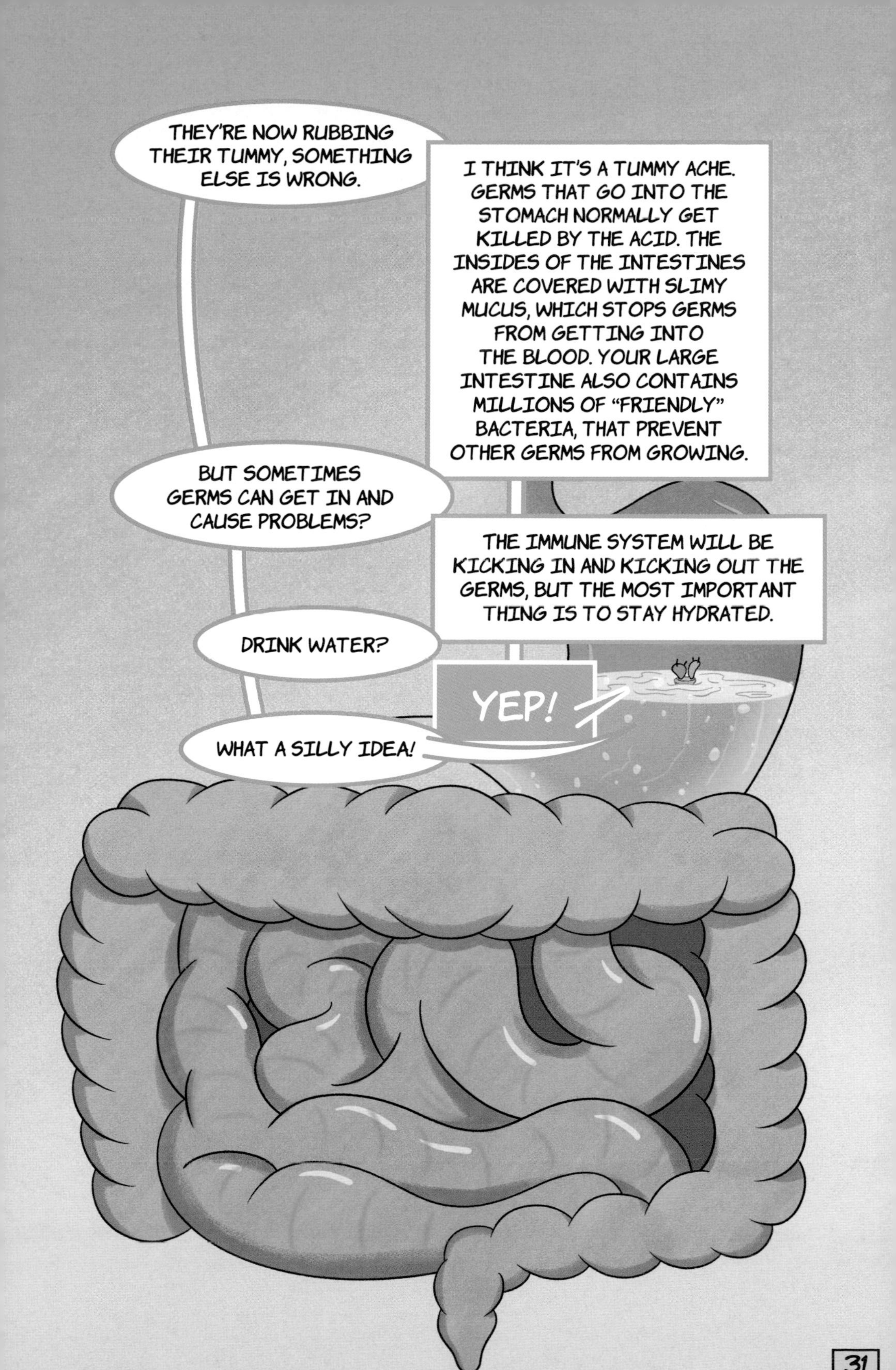
THEY'RE NOW RUBBING THEIR TUMMY, SOMETHING ELSE IS WRONG.
I THINK IT'S A TUMMY ACHE. GERMS THAT GO INTO THE STOMACH NORMALLY GET KILLED BY THE ACID. THE INSIDES OF THE INTESTINES ARE COVERED WITH SLIMY MUCUS, WHICH STOPS GERMS FROM GETTING INTO THE BLOOD. YOUR LARGE INTESTINE ALSO CONTAINS MILLIONS OF "FRIENDLY" BACTERIA, THAT PREVENT OTHER GERMS FROM GROWING.
BUT SOMETIMES GERMS CAN GET IN AND CAUSE PROBLEMS?
THE IMMUNE SYSTEM WILL BE KICKING IN AND KICKING OUT THE GERMS, BUT THE MOST IMPORTANT THING IS TO STAY HYDRATED.
DRINK WATER?
YEP!
WHAT A SILLY IDEA!

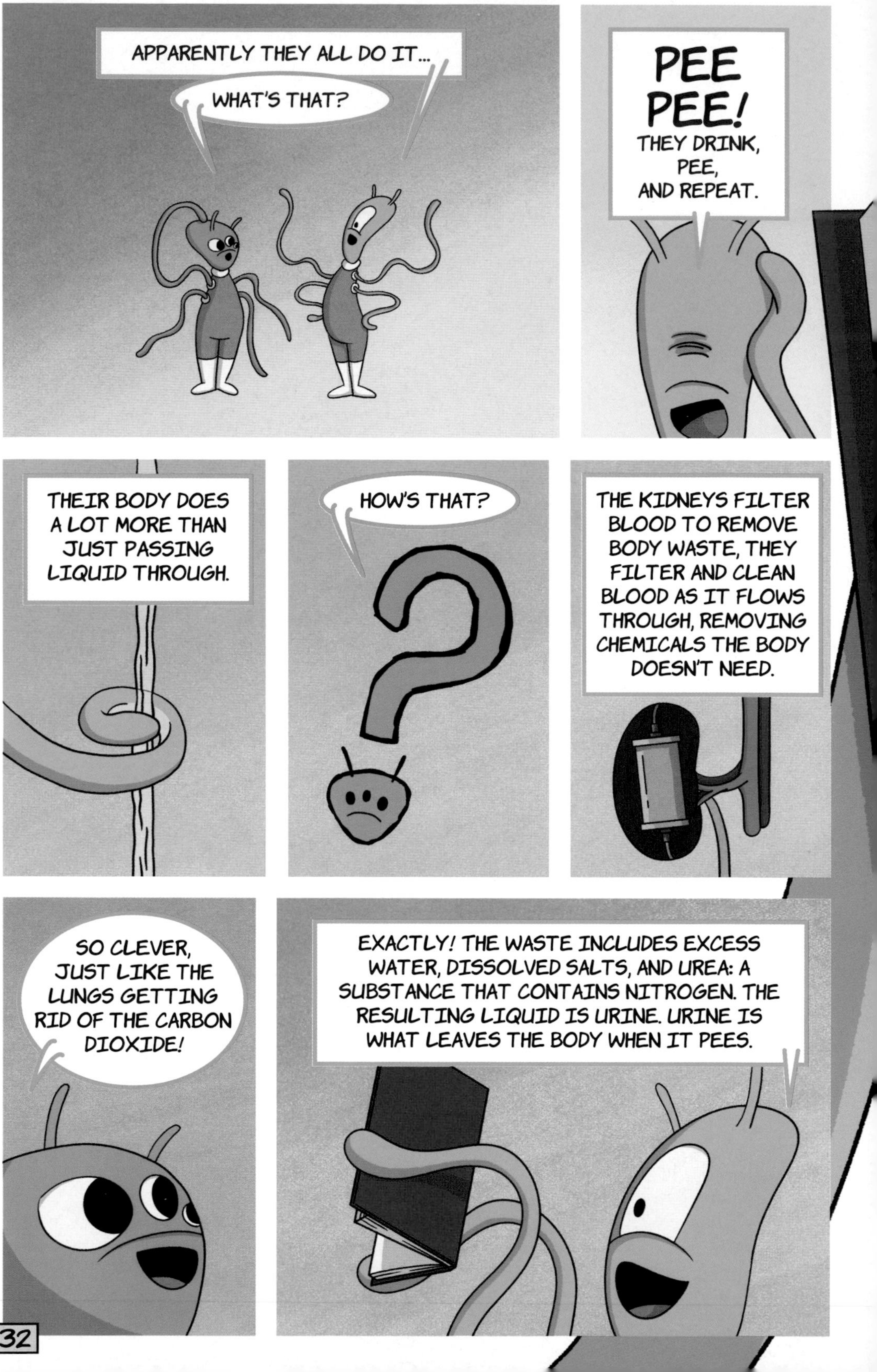
APPARENTLY THEY ALL DO IT...
WHAT'S THAT?
PEE PEE! THEY DRINK, PEE, AND REPEAT.
THEIR BODY DOES A LOT MORE THAN JUST PASSING LIQUID THROUGH.
HOW'S THAT?
THE KIDNEYS FILTER BLOOD TO REMOVE BODY WASTE, THEY FILTER AND CLEAN BLOOD AS IT FLOWS THROUGH, REMOVING CHEMICALS THE BODY DOESN'T NEED.
SO CLEVER, JUST LIKE THE LUNGS GETTING RID OF THE CARBON DIOXIDE!
EXACTLY! THE WASTE INCLUDES EXCESS WATER, DISSOLVED SALTS, AND UREA: A SUBSTANCE THAT CONTAINS NITROGEN. THE RESULTING LIQUID IS URINE. URINE IS WHAT LEAVES THE BODY WHEN IT PEES.

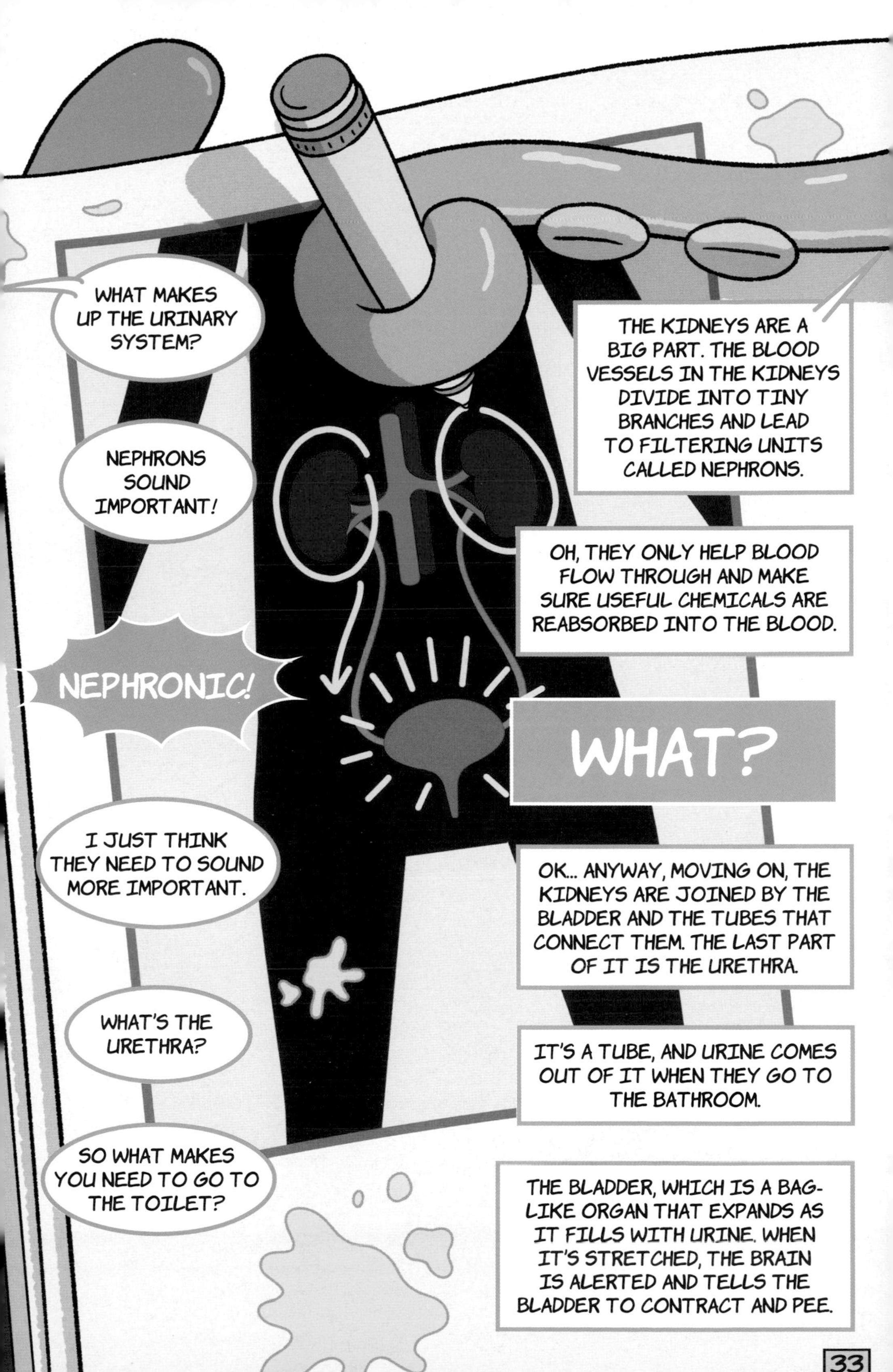
WHAT MAKES UP THE URINARY SYSTEM?
THE KIDNEYS ARE A BIG PART. THE BLOOD VESSELS IN THE KIDNEYS DIVIDE INTO TINY BRANCHES AND LEAD TO FILTERING UNITS CALLED NEPHRONS.
NEPHRONS SOUND IMPORTANT!
OH, THEY ONLY HELP BLOOD FLOW THROUGH AND MAKE SURE USEFUL CHEMICALS ARE REABSORBED INTO THE BLOOD.
NEPHRONIC!
WHAT?
I JUST THINK THEY NEED TO SOUND MORE IMPORTANT.
OK... ANYWAY, MOVING ON, THE KIDNEYS ARE JOINED BY THE BLADDER AND THE TUBES THAT CONNECT THEM. THE LAST PART OF IT IS THE URETHRA.
WHAT'S THE URETHRA?
IT'S A TUBE, AND URINE COMES OUT OF IT WHEN THEY GO TO THE BATHROOM.
SO WHAT MAKES YOU NEED TO GO TO THE TOILET?
THE BLADDER, WHICH IS A BAG-LIKE ORGAN THAT EXPANDS AS IT FILLS WITH URINE. WHEN IT'S STRETCHED, THE BRAIN IS ALERTED AND TELLS THE BLADDER TO CONTRACT AND PEE.

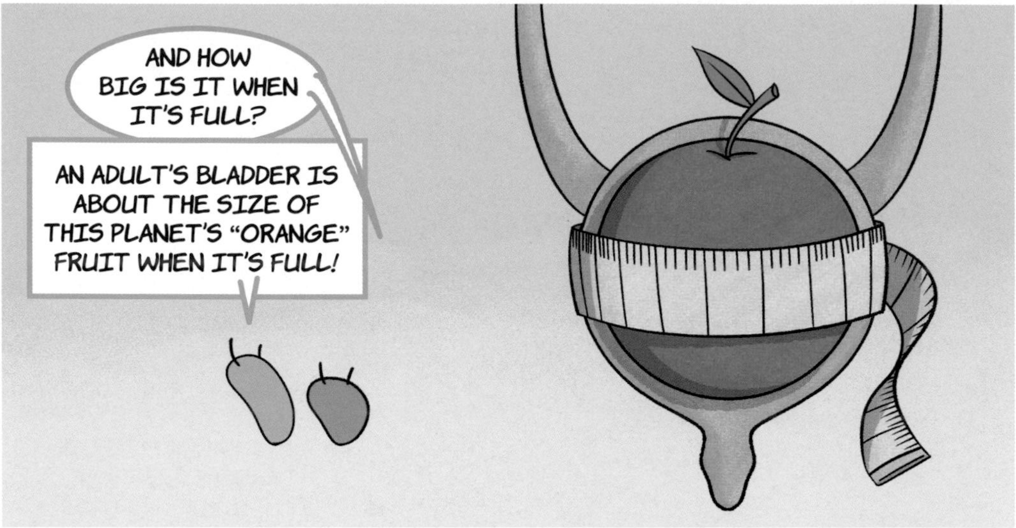
AND HOW BIG IS IT WHEN IT'S FULL?
AN ADULT'S BLADDER IS ABOUT THE SIZE OF THIS PLANET'S "ORANGE" FRUIT WHEN IT'S FULL!

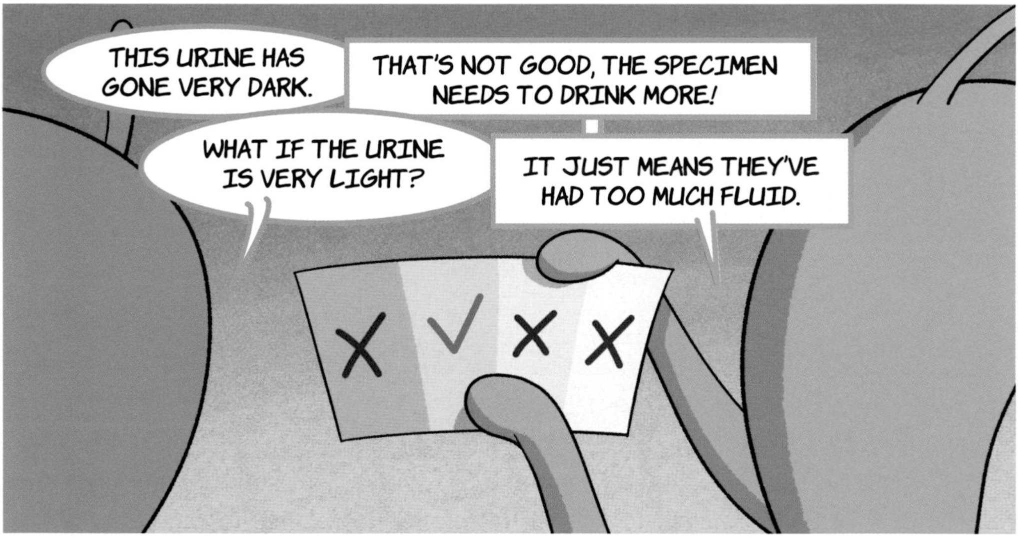
THIS URINE HAS GONE VERY DARK.
THAT'S NOT GOOD, THE SPECIMEN NEEDS TO DRINK MORE!
WHAT IF THE URINE IS VERY LIGHT?
IT JUST MEANS THEY'VE HAD TOO MUCH FLUID.

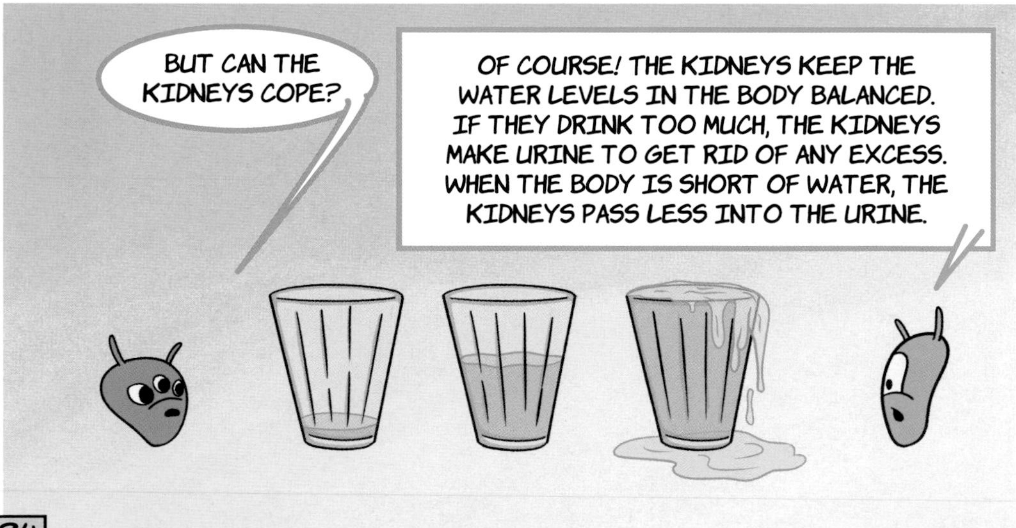
BUT CAN THE KIDNEYS COPE?
OF COURSE! THE KIDNEYS KEEP THE WATER LEVELS IN THE BODY BALANCED. IF THEY DRINK TOO MUCH, THE KIDNEYS MAKE URINE TO GET RID OF ANY EXCESS. WHEN THE BODY IS SHORT OF WATER, THE KIDNEYS PASS LESS INTO THE URINE.

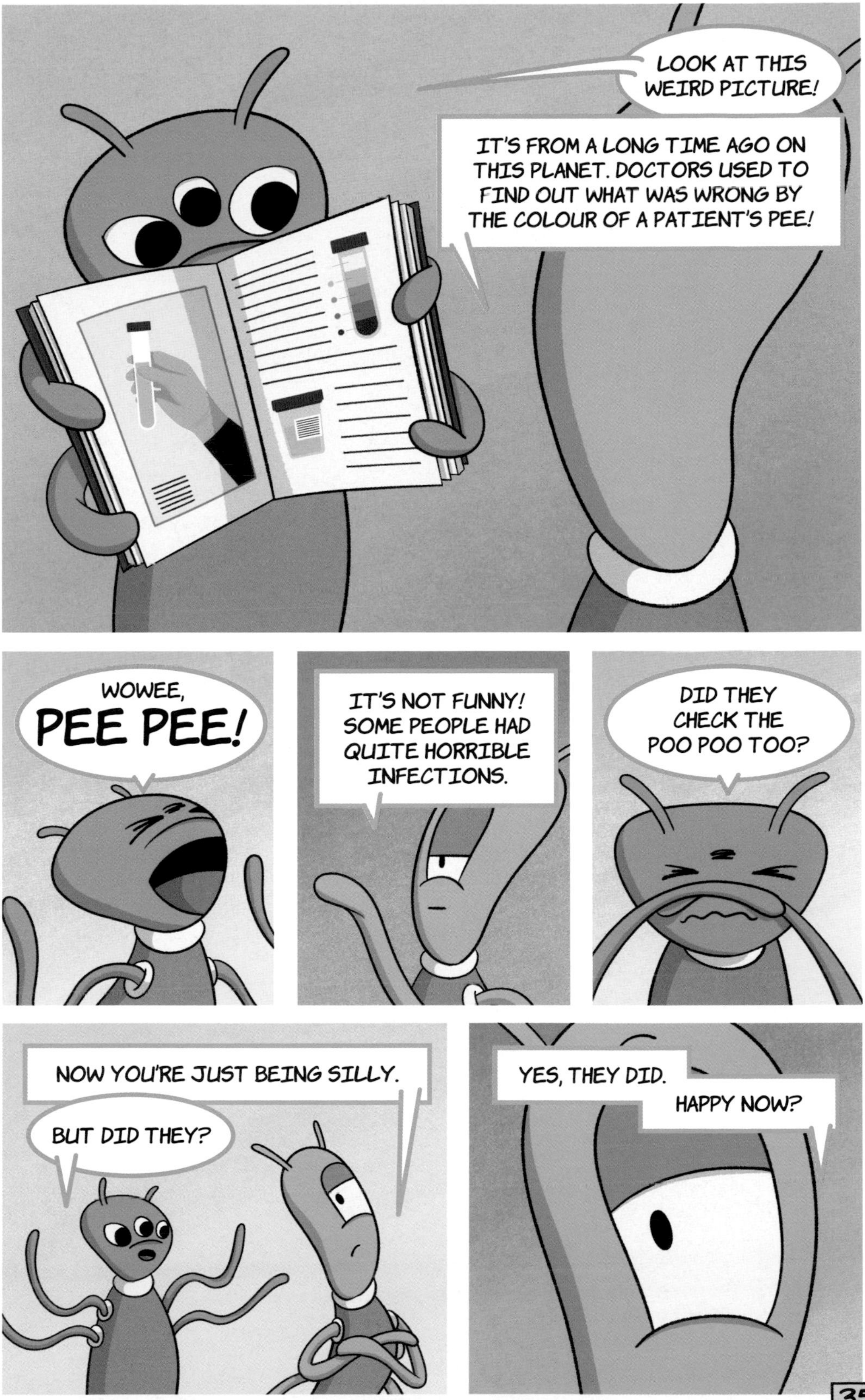
LOOK AT THIS WEIRD PICTURE!
IT'S FROM A LONG TIME AGO ON THIS PLANET. DOCTORS USED TO FIND OUT WHAT WAS WRONG BY THE COLOUR OF A PATIENT'S PEE!
WOWEE, PEE PEE!
IT'S NOT FUNNY! SOME PEOPLE HAD QUITE HORRIBLE INFECTIONS.
DID THEY CHECK THE POO POO TOO?
NOW YOU'RE JUST BEING SILLY.
BUT DID THEY?
YES, THEY DID.
HAPPY NOW?

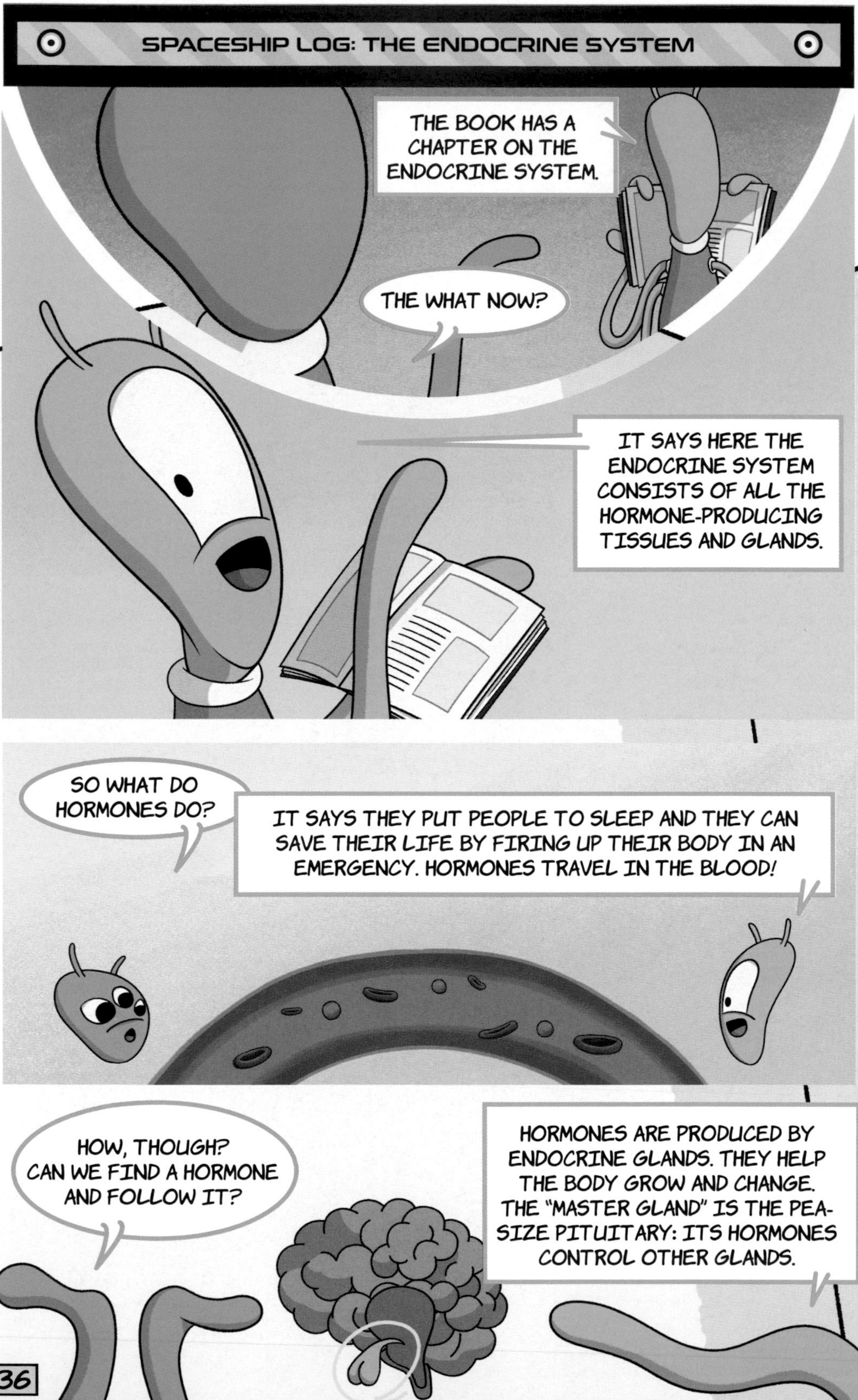
SPACESHIP LOG: THE ENDOCRINE SYSTEM
THE BOOK HAS A CHAPTER ON THE ENDOCRINE SYSTEM.
THE WHAT NOW?
IT SAYS HERE THE ENDOCRINE SYSTEM CONSISTS OF ALL THE HORMONE-PRODUCING TISSUES AND GLANDS.
SO WHAT DO HORMONES DO?
IT SAYS THEY PUT PEOPLE TO SLEEP AND THEY CAN SAVE THEIR LIFE BY FIRING UP THEIR BODY IN AN EMERGENCY. HORMONES TRAVEL IN THE BLOOD!
HOW, THOUGH? CAN WE FIND A HORMONE AND FOLLOW IT?
HORMONES ARE PRODUCED BY ENDOCRINE GLANDS. THEY HELP THE BODY GROW AND CHANGE. THE "MASTER GLAND" IS THE PEA-SIZE PITUITARY: ITS HORMONES CONTROL OTHER GLANDS.

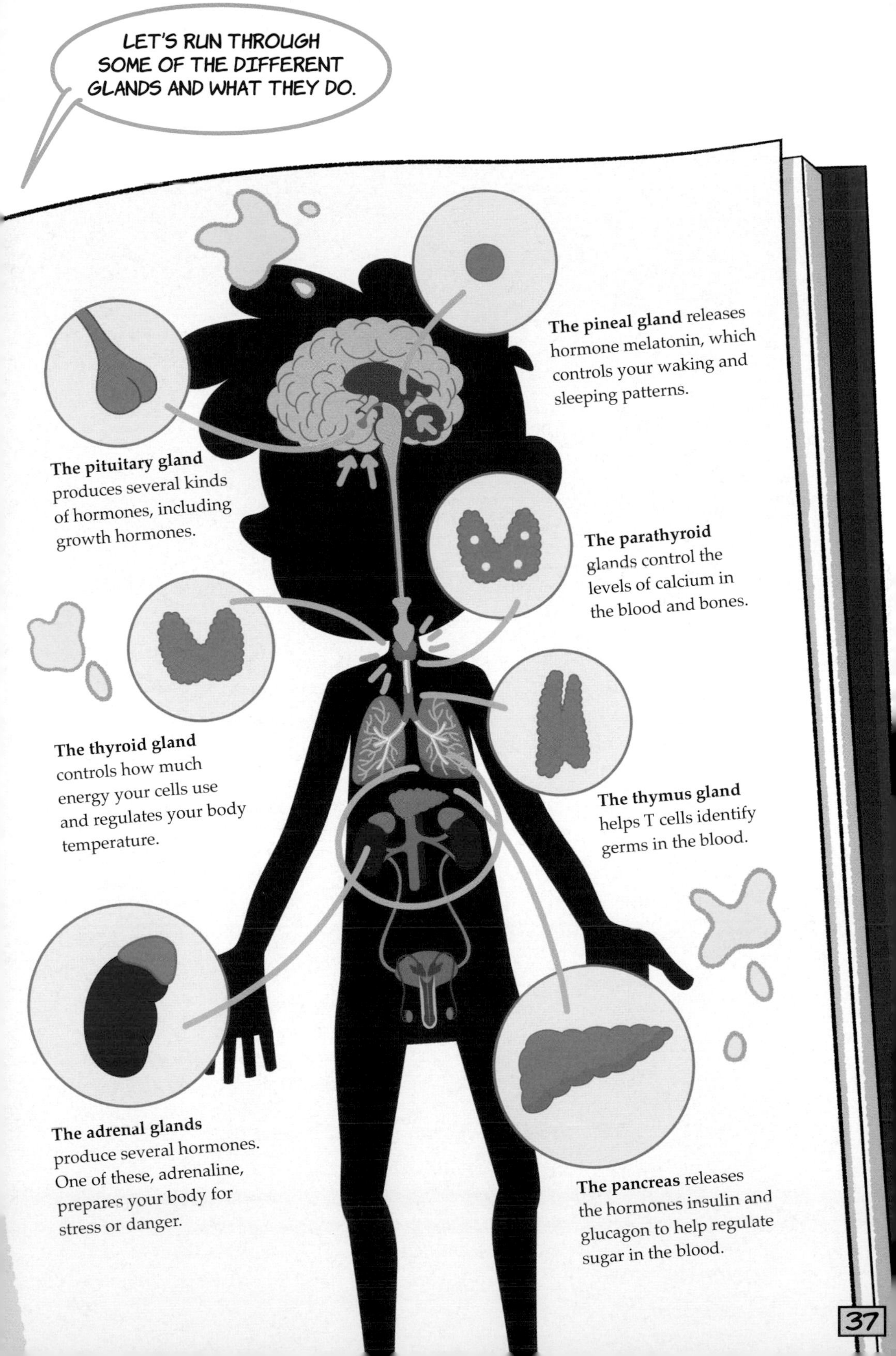
LET'S RUN THROUGH SOME OF THE DIFFERENT GLANDS AND WHAT THEY DO.
The pineal gland releases hormone melatonin, which controls your waking and sleeping patterns.
The pituitary gland produces several kinds of hormones, including growth hormones.
The parathyroid glands control the levels of calcium in the blood and bones.
The thyroid gland controls how much energy your cells use and regulates your body temperature.
The thymus gland helps T cells identify germs in the blood.
The adrenal glands produce several hormones. One of these, adrenaline, prepares your body for stress or danger.
The pancreas releases the hormones insulin and glucagon to help regulate sugar in the blood.

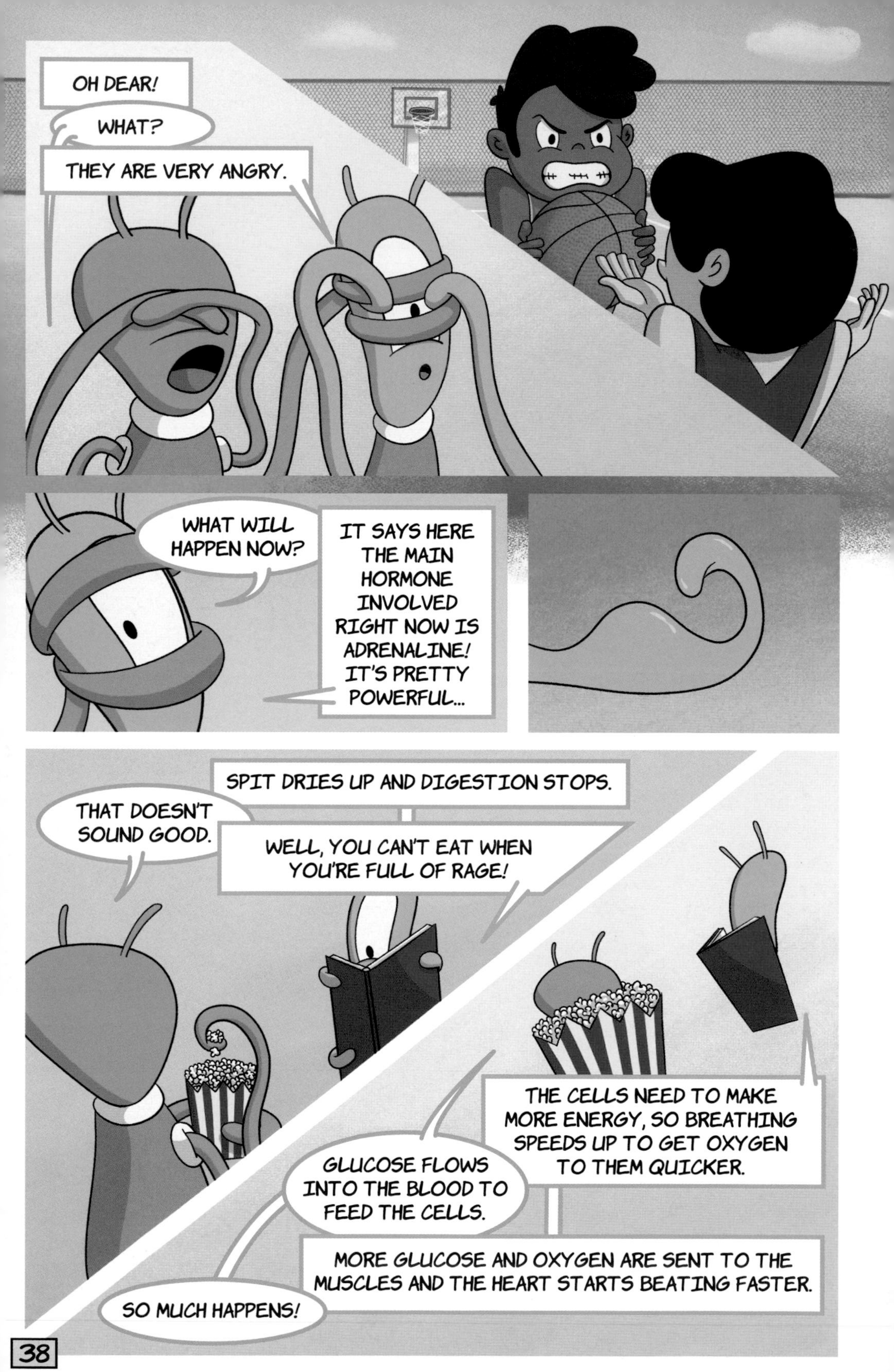

OH DEAR!
WHAT?
THEY ARE VERY ANGRY.
WHAT WILL HAPPEN NOW?
IT SAYS HERE THE MAIN HORMONE INVOLVED RIGHT NOW IS ADRENALINE! IT'S PRETTY POWERFUL...
SPIT DRIES UP AND DIGESTION STOPS.
THAT DOESN'T SOUND GOOD.
WELL, YOU CAN'T EAT WHEN YOU'RE FULL OF RAGE!
THE CELLS NEED TO MAKE MORE ENERGY, SO BREATHING SPEEDS UP TO GET OXYGEN TO THEM QUICKER.
GLUCOSE FLOWS INTO THE BLOOD TO FEED THE CELLS.
MORE GLUCOSE AND OXYGEN ARE SENT TO THE MUSCLES AND THE HEART STARTS BEATING FASTER.
SO MUCH HAPPENS!

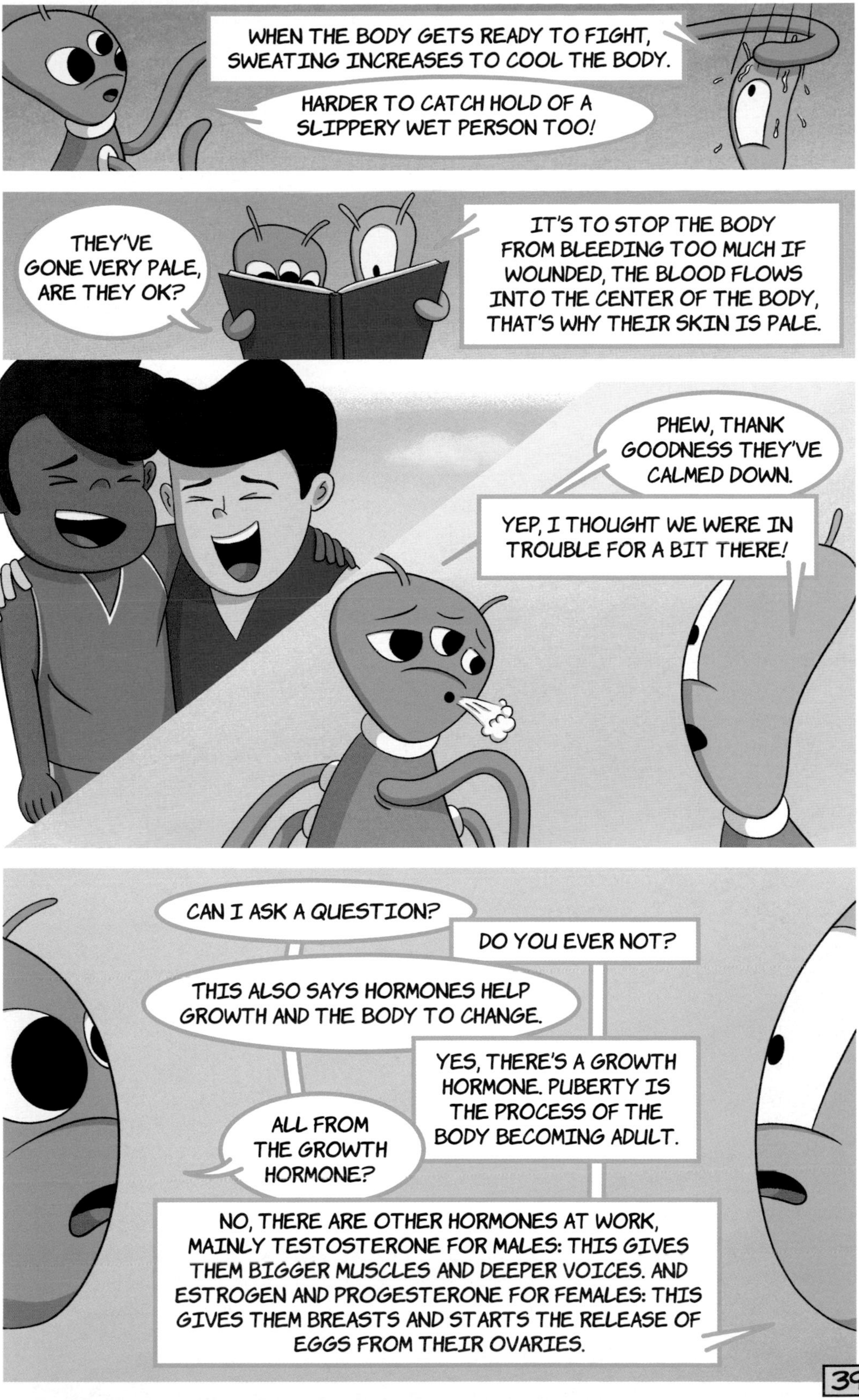
WHEN THE BODY GETS READY TO FIGHT, SWEATING INCREASES TO COOL THE BODY.
HARDER TO CATCH HOLD OF A SLIPPERY WET PERSON TOO!
THEY'VE GONE VERY PALE, ARE THEY OK?
IT'S TO STOP THE BODY FROM BLEEDING TOO MUCH IF WOUNDED, THE BLOOD FLOWS INTO THE CENTER OF THE BODY, THAT'S WHY THEIR SKIN IS PALE.
PHEW, THANK GOODNESS THEY'VE CALMED DOWN.
YEP, I THOUGHT WE WERE IN TROUBLE FOR A BIT THERE!
CAN I ASK A QUESTION?
DO YOU EVER NOT?
THIS ALSO SAYS HORMONES HELP GROWTH AND THE BODY TO CHANGE.
YES, THERE'S A GROWTH HORMONE. PUBERTY IS THE PROCESS OF THE BODY BECOMING ADULT.
ALL FROM THE GROWTH HORMONE?
NO, THERE ARE OTHER HORMONES AT WORK, MAINLY TESTOSTERONE FOR MALES: THIS GIVES THEM BIGGER MUSCLES AND DEEPER VOICES. AND ESTROGEN AND PROGESTERONE FOR FEMALES: THIS GIVES THEM BREASTS AND STARTS THE RELEASE OF EGGS FROM THEIR OVARIES.

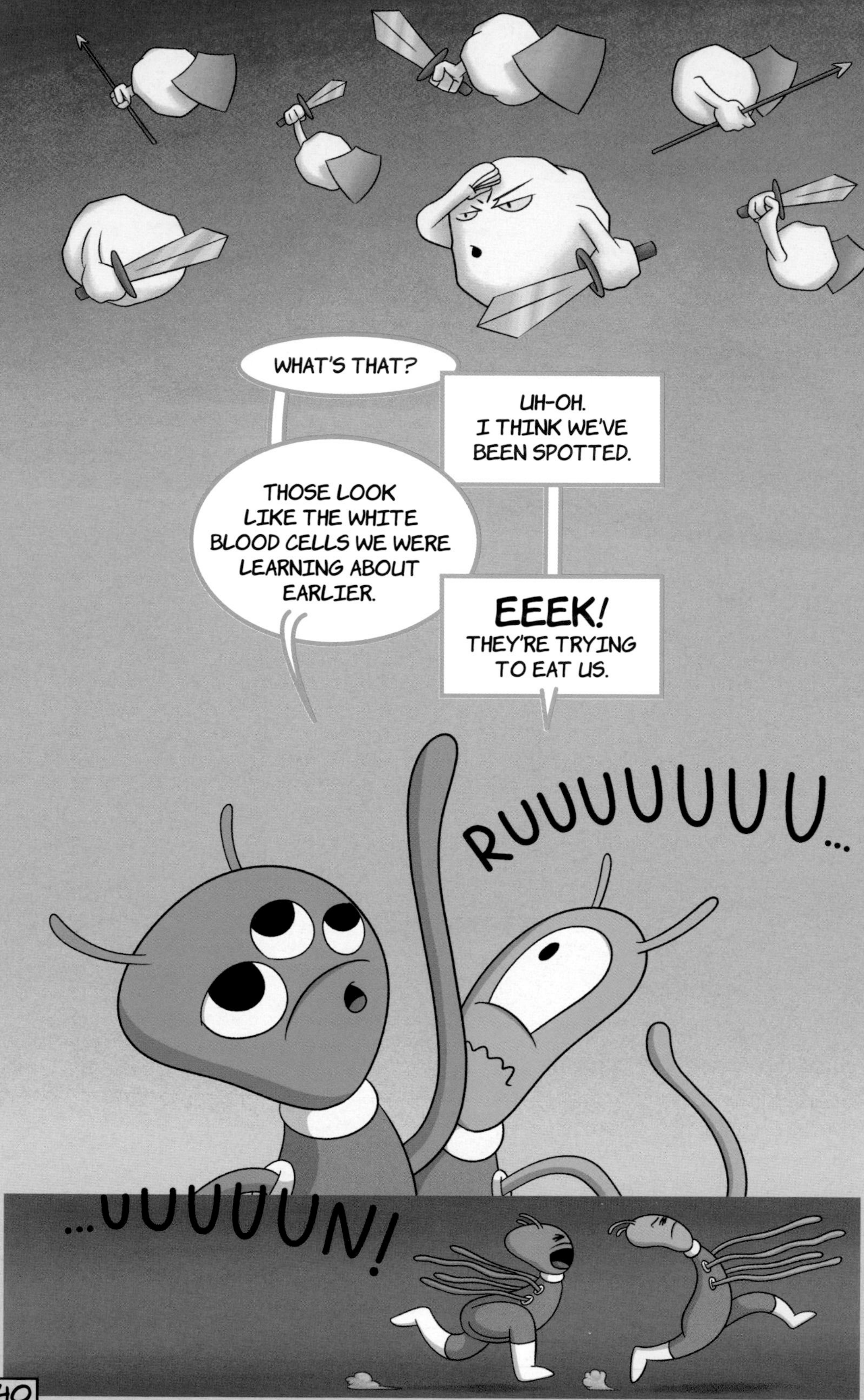
WHAT'S THAT?
UH-OH. I THINK WE'VE BEEN SPOTTED.
THOSE LOOK LIKE THE WHITE BLOOD CELLS WE WERE LEARNING ABOUT EARLIER.
EEEK! THEY'RE TRYING TO EAT US.
RUUUUUUUU...
...UUUUUN!

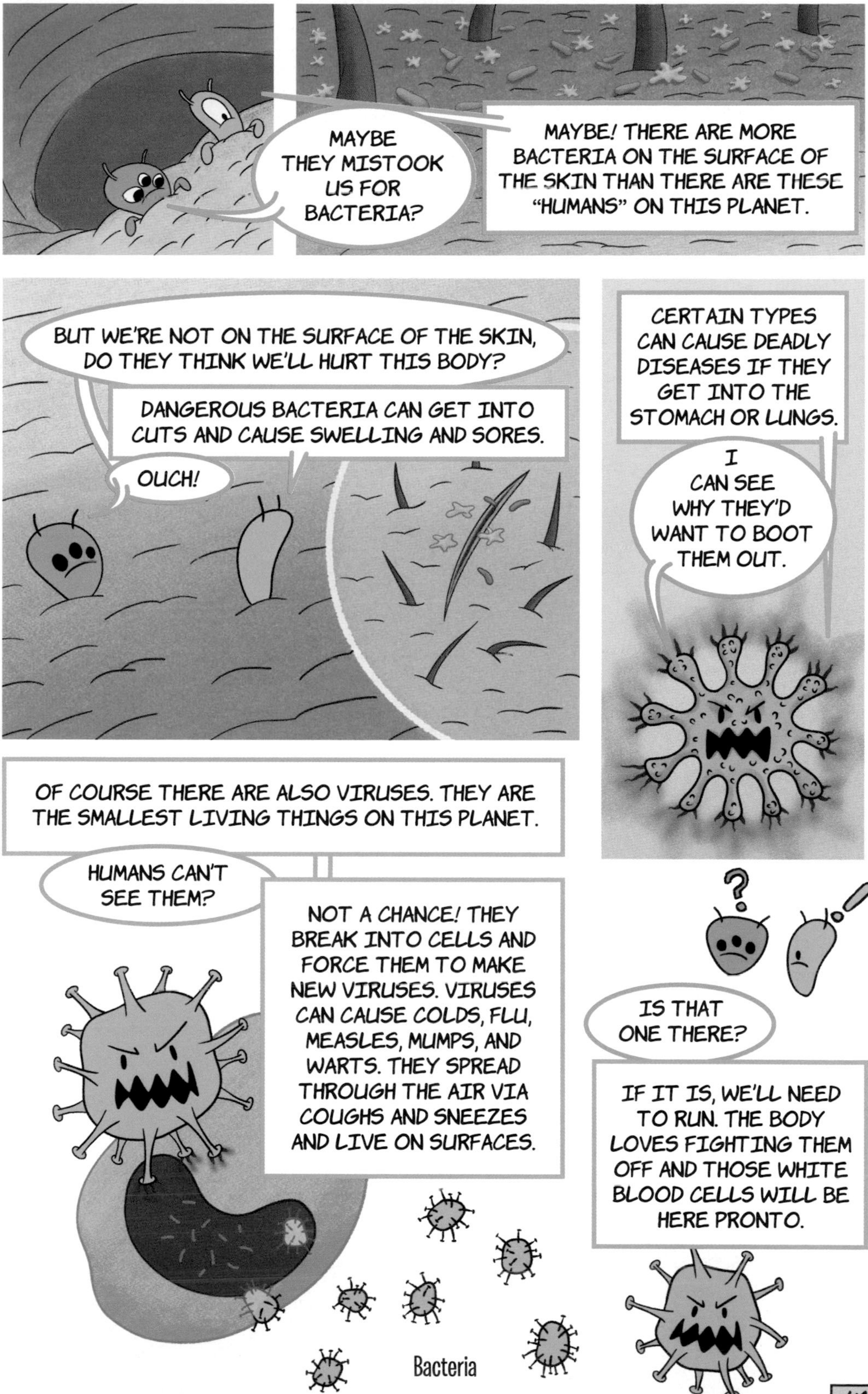
MAYBE THEY MISTOOK US FOR BACTERIA?
MAYBE! THERE ARE MORE BACTERIA ON THE SURFACE OF THE SKIN THAN THERE ARE THESE "HUMANS" ON THIS PLANET.
BUT WE'RE NOT ON THE SURFACE OF THE SKIN, DO THEY THINK WE'LL HURT THIS BODY?
DANGEROUS BACTERIA CAN GET INTO CUTS AND CAUSE SWELLING AND SORES.
OUCH!
CERTAIN TYPES CAN CAUSE DEADLY DISEASES IF THEY GET INTO THE STOMACH OR LUNGS.
I CAN SEE WHY THEY'D WANT TO BOOT THEM OUT.
OF COURSE THERE ARE ALSO VIRUSES. THEY ARE THE SMALLEST LIVING THINGS ON THIS PLANET.
HUMANS CAN'T SEE THEM?
NOT A CHANCE! THEY BREAK INTO CELLS AND FORCE THEM TO MAKE NEW VIRUSES. VIRUSES CAN CAUSE COLDS, FLU, MEASLES, MUMPS, AND WARTS. THEY SPREAD THROUGH THE AIR VIA COUGHS AND SNEEZES AND LIVE ON SURFACES.
?
!
IS THAT ONE THERE?
IF IT IS, WE'LL NEED TO RUN. THE BODY LOVES FIGHTING THEM OFF AND THOSE WHITE BLOOD CELLS WILL BE HERE PRONTO.
Bacteria

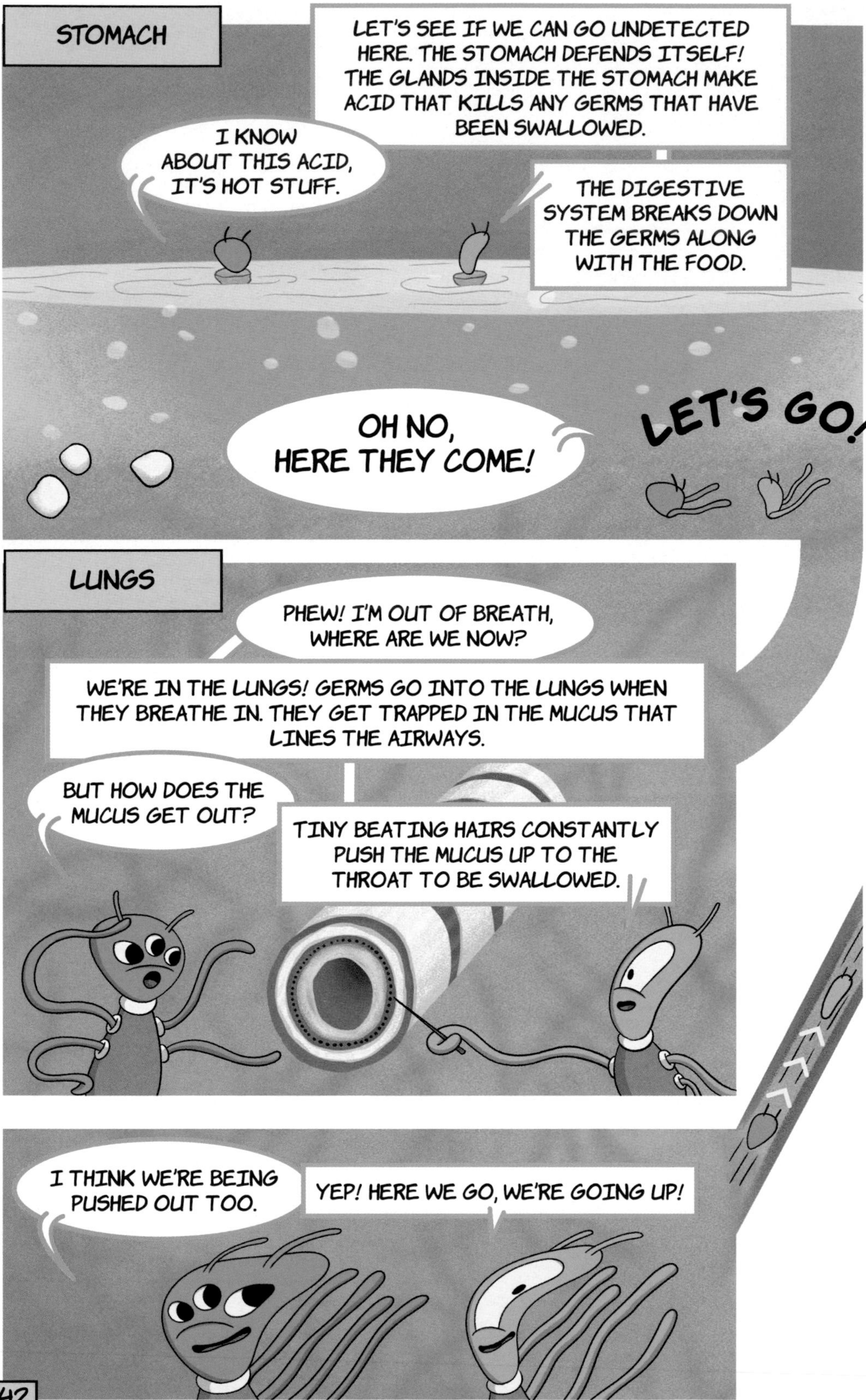
STOMACH
LET'S SEE IF WE CAN GO UNDETECTED HERE. THE STOMACH DEFENDS ITSELF! THE GLANDS INSIDE THE STOMACH MAKE ACID THAT KILLS ANY GERMS THAT HAVE BEEN SWALLOWED.
I KNOW ABOUT THIS ACID, IT'S HOT STUFF.
THE DIGESTIVE SYSTEM BREAKS DOWN THE GERMS ALONG WITH THE FOOD.
OH NO, HERE THEY COME!
LET'S GO!
LUNGS
PHEW! I'M OUT OF BREATH, WHERE ARE WE NOW?
WE'RE IN THE LUNGS! GERMS GO INTO THE LUNGS WHEN THEY BREATHE IN. THEY GET TRAPPED IN THE MUCUS THAT LINES THE AIRWAYS.
BUT HOW DOES THE MUCUS GET OUT?
TINY BEATING HAIRS CONSTANTLY PUSH THE MUCUS UP TO THE THROAT TO BE SWALLOWED.
I THINK WE'RE BEING PUSHED OUT TOO.
YEP! HERE WE GO, WE'RE GOING UP!

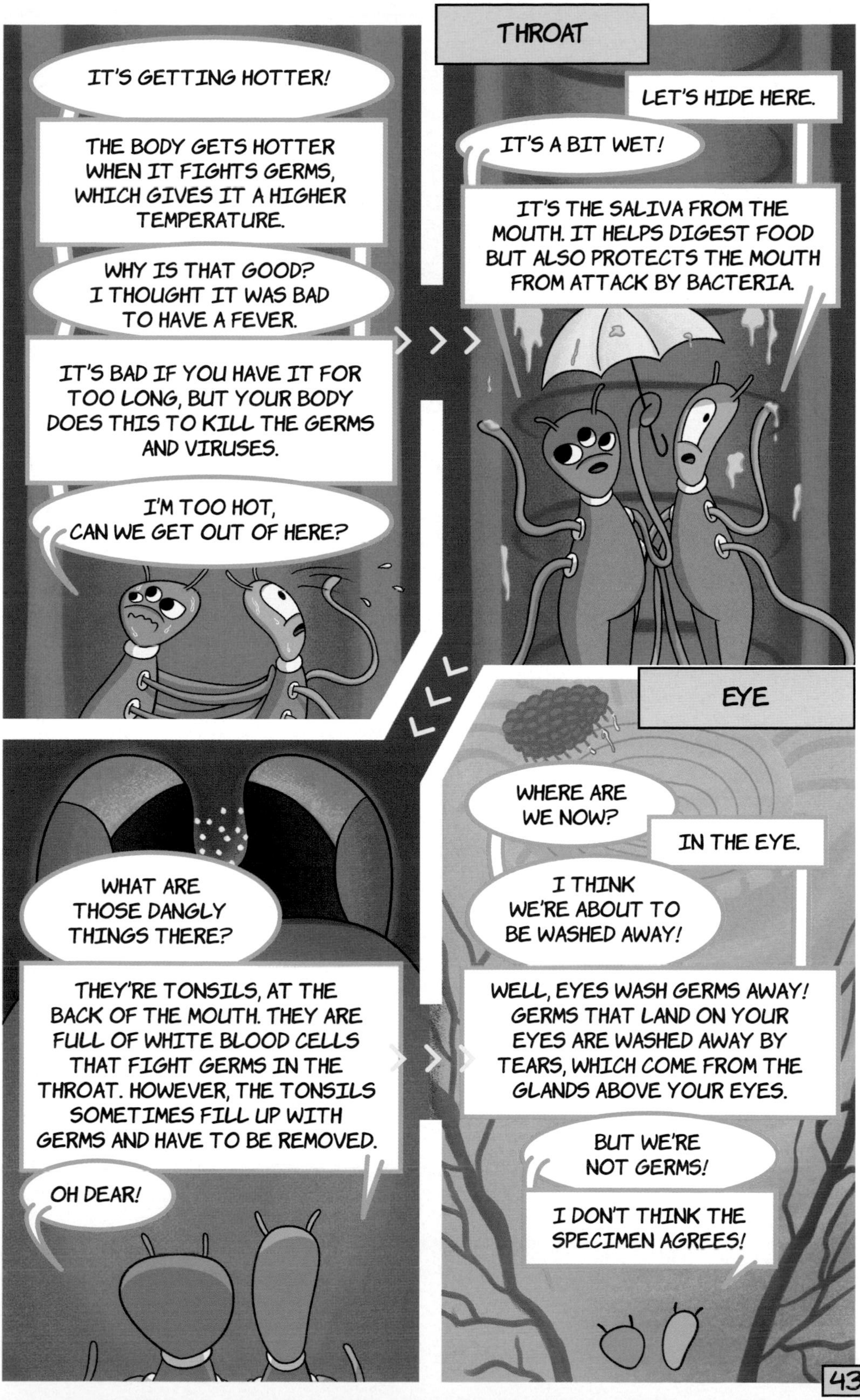
IT'S GETTING HOTTER!
THE BODY GETS HOTTER WHEN IT FIGHTS GERMS, WHICH GIVES IT A HIGHER TEMPERATURE.
WHY IS THAT GOOD? I THOUGHT IT WAS BAD TO HAVE A FEVER.
IT'S BAD IF YOU HAVE IT FOR TOO LONG, BUT YOUR BODY DOES THIS TO KILL THE GERMS AND VIRUSES.
I'M TOO HOT, CAN WE GET OUT OF HERE?
THROAT
LET'S HIDE HERE.
IT'S A BIT WET!
IT'S THE SALIVA FROM THE MOUTH. IT HELPS DIGEST FOOD BUT ALSO PROTECTS THE MOUTH FROM ATTACK BY BACTERIA.
WHAT ARE THOSE DANGLY THINGS THERE?
THEY'RE TONSILS, AT THE BACK OF THE MOUTH. THEY ARE FULL OF WHITE BLOOD CELLS THAT FIGHT GERMS IN THE THROAT. HOWEVER, THE TONSILS SOMETIMES FILL UP WITH GERMS AND HAVE TO BE REMOVED.
OH DEAR!
EYE
WHERE ARE WE NOW?
IN THE EYE.
I THINK WE'RE ABOUT TO BE WASHED AWAY!
WELL, EYES WASH GERMS AWAY! GERMS THAT LAND ON YOUR EYES ARE WASHED AWAY BY TEARS, WHICH COME FROM THE GLANDS ABOVE YOUR EYES.
BUT WE'RE NOT GERMS!
I DON'T THINK THE SPECIMEN AGREES!

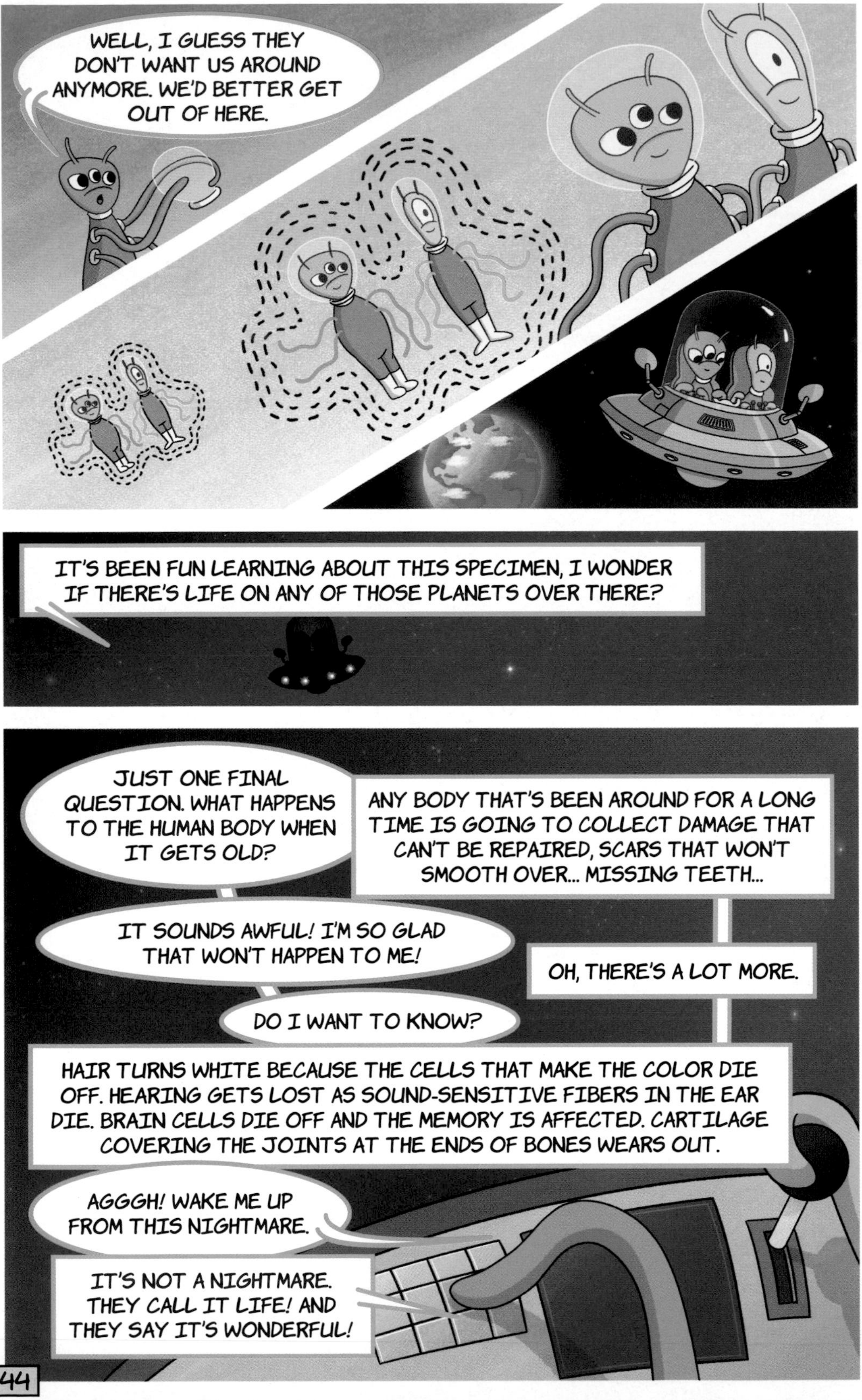
WELL, I GUESS THEY DON'T WANT US AROUND ANYMORE. WE'D BETTER GET OUT OF HERE.
IT'S BEEN FUN LEARNING ABOUT THIS SPECIMEN, I WONDER IF THERE'S LIFE ON ANY OF THOSE PLANETS OVER THERE?
JUST ONE FINAL QUESTION. WHAT HAPPENS TO THE HUMAN BODY WHEN IT GETS OLD?
ANY BODY THAT'S BEEN AROUND FOR A LONG TIME IS GOING TO COLLECT DAMAGE THAT CAN'T BE REPAIRED, SCARS THAT WON'T SMOOTH OVER... MISSING TEETH...
IT SOUNDS AWFUL! I'M SO GLAD THAT WON'T HAPPEN TO ME!
OH, THERE'S A LOT MORE.
DO I WANT TO KNOW?
HAIR TURNS WHITE BECAUSE THE CELLS THAT MAKE THE COLOR DIE OFF. HEARING GETS LOST AS SOUND-SENSITIVE FIBERS IN THE EAR DIE. BRAIN CELLS DIE OFF AND THE MEMORY IS AFFECTED. CARTILAGE COVERING THE JOINTS AT THE ENDS OF BONES WEARS OUT.
AGGGH! WAKE ME UP FROM THIS NIGHTMARE.
IT'S NOT A NIGHTMARE. THEY CALL IT LIFE! AND THEY SAY IT'S WONDERFUL!

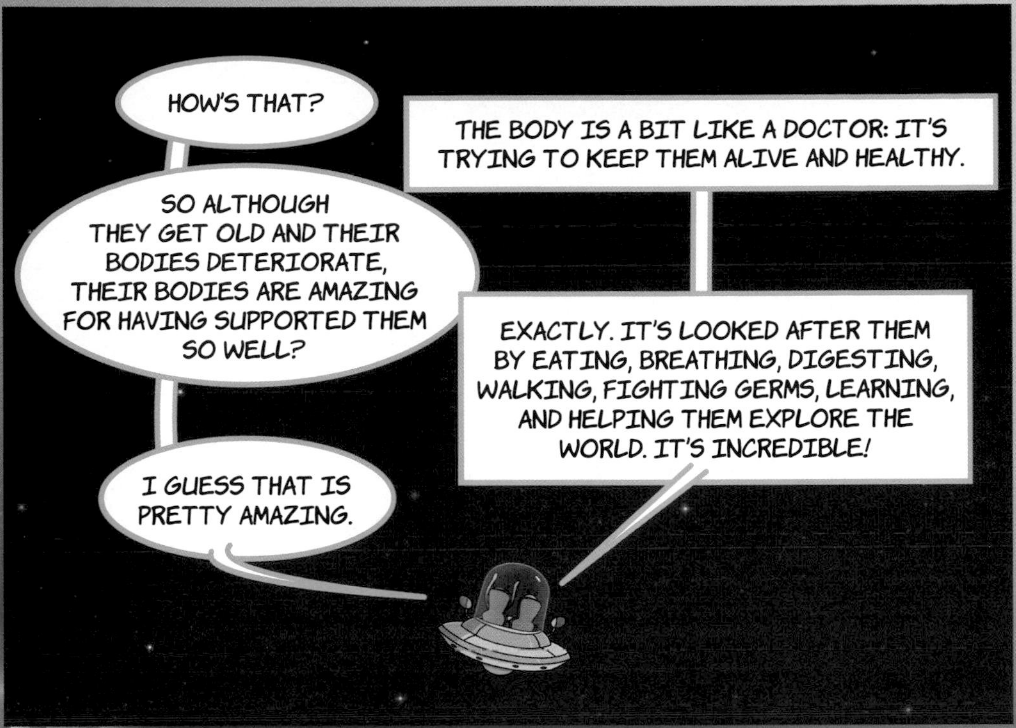
HOW'S THAT?
THE BODY IS A BIT LIKE A DOCTOR: IT'S TRYING TO KEEP THEM ALIVE AND HEALTHY.
SO ALTHOUGH THEY GET OLD AND THEIR BODIES DETERIORATE, THEIR BODIES ARE AMAZING FOR HAVING SUPPORTED THEM SO WELL?
EXACTLY. IT'S LOOKED AFTER THEM BY EATING, BREATHING, DIGESTING, WALKING, FIGHTING GERMS, LEARNING, AND HELPING THEM EXPLORE THE WORLD. IT'S INCREDIBLE!
I GUESS THAT IS PRETTY AMAZING.

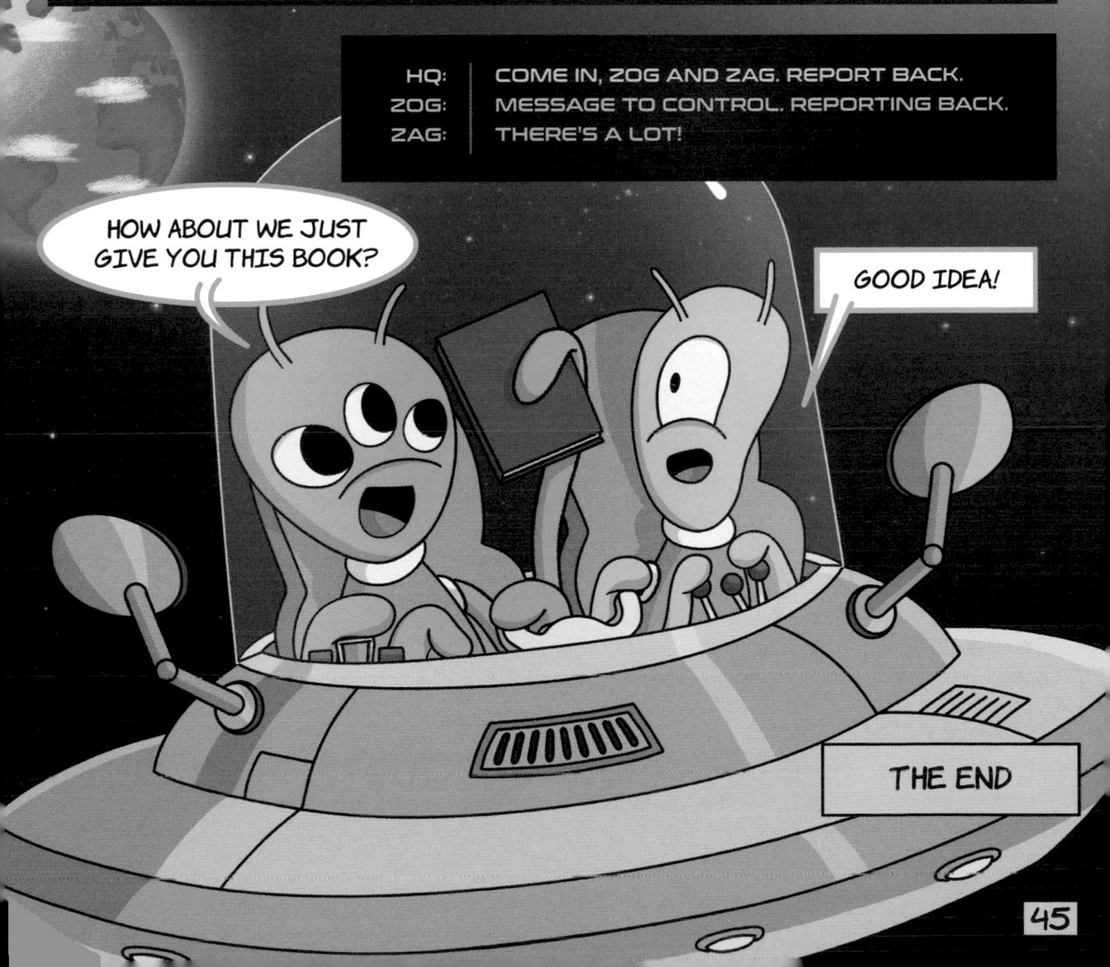
HQ: COME IN, ZOG AND ZAG. REPORT BACK.
ZOG: MESSAGE TO CONTROL. REPORTING BACK.
ZAG: THERE'S A LOT!
HOW ABOUT WE JUST GIVE YOU THIS BOOK?
GOOD IDEA!
THE END

GLOSSARY

adrenal gland: a gland near the kidneys that makes adrenaline

antibodies: chemicals in the body that destroy or disable germs

arteries: blood vessels that carry blood away from the heart

bacteria: a type of microorganism; some cause diseases but some are harmless or even useful

capillaries: tiny blood vessels that deliver oxygen and food to cells, and carry waste products away

carbon dioxide: a gas that cells make as a waste product. It is carried by the lungs to be breathed out

cell: a tiny living unit. Cells make up the bodies of living things. The human body is made up of millions of cells.

circulatory system: the organs and tubes that circulate blood around the body, including the heart and blood vessels

digestive system: a set of organs and body parts that breaks down food, extracts useful chemicals from it, and carries waste out of the body

endocrine system: a set of glands that release hormones to control the way the body works

enzyme: a substance that speeds up chemical reactions such as those that break down food during digestion

germ: a microorganism, such as a bacterium or virus, that causes disease

glands: small organs that release chemicals that help the body work

hormones: chemicals that the body releases into the bloodstream to control various functions

immune system: a set of organs and body parts that fight germs or dirt that gets into the body

intestines: long tubes that form part of the digestive system. There are two types: the small intestine and the large intestine.

kidney: an organ that filters waste chemicals from the blood and controls the amount of water in the body. Most people have two kidneys.

joints: any points where two bones link together

lymphocytes: a type of white blood cell

mucus: a slimy substance made in some parts of the body, such as the nose and the stomach

muscular system: the set of muscles that make your body move

nerves: bundles of fibers that carry messages from your brain and spinal cord to the rest of your body

nervous system: the nerves, brain, and spinal cord, which control and carry messages around your body

oxygen: a gas found in the air; humans need to take in oxygen to make their bodies work

plasma: a liquid that is one of the main components of blood

platelet: a type of cell fragment found in blood, used by the body to make blood clots

puberty: a stage of development when a child becomes an adult

red blood cells: cells that carry oxygen around the body

respiratory system: a of organs that allow you to breathe in oxygen and breathe out waste gases

saliva: a liquid released into the mouth to dissolve food and make it easier to swallow

skeletal muscles: muscles that are connected to the skeleton

spine: the column of 33 bones, called vertebrae, that forms the central part of the skeleton

stomach: a strong stretchy bag that receives chewed food; the stomach breaks down the food by squeezing it and dissolving it with acid